Confessions of a Jewish Shiksa

Confessions of a Jewish Shiksa

By

Frannie Sheridan

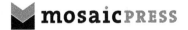

Library and Archives Canada Cataloguing in Publication

Title: Confessions of a Jewish shiksa: the second greatest story ever told /
            Frannie Sheridan.

Names: Sheridan, Frannie, 1961- author.

Identifiers: Canadiana (print) 20200298208
                Canadiana (ebook) 20200298291

ISBN 9781771614962 (softcover) | ISBN 9781771614986 (EPUB) |
ISBN 9781771614979 (PDF) | ISBN 9781771614993 (Kindle)

Subjects: LCSH: Sheridan, Frannie, 1961- | LCSH: Children of Holocaust survivors—
            Canada—Biography. | LCSH: Jewish women—Canada—Biography.
            LCSH: Jewish women authors—Canada—Biography. | LCSH: Family
            violence. | LCSH: Psychic trauma. | CSH: Women authors, Canadian
            (English)—Biography. | LCGFT: Autobiographies.

Classification: LCC PS8587.H3854 Z46 2020
                  DDC C818/.5403—dc23

Published by Mosaic Press, Oakville, Ontario, Canada, 2021.

MOSAIC PRESS, Publishers
www.Mosaic-Press.com
Copyright © Mosaic Press

Cover design by Rahim Piracha.

ONTARIO ARTS COUNCIL
CONSEIL DES ARTS DE L'ONTARIO
an Ontario government agency
un organisme du gouvernement de l'Ontario

Funded by the Government of Canada
Financé par le gouvernement du Canada | Canadä

ONTARIO
CREATES

MOSAIC PRESS
1252 Speers Road, Units 1 & 2, Oakville, Ontario, L6L 5N9
(905) 825-2130 • info@mosaic-press.com • www.mosaic-press.com

SHIKSA is Yiddish for a non-Jewish woman.
NOT a two-wheeled vehicle drawn by one or more Jews.
That is a Jewish rickshaw.

NOTE: Pseudonyms have been used in place of the actual names of my siblings to increase my chances of being invited to future family kvetch-sessions, I mean get-togethers.

Foreword

I have known the incomparable actor, playwright and comedian, Frannie Sheridan for almost 25 years, since I first investigated the seemingly incredible details of her family's secret past that she was revealing on stage, one gag at a time. I followed the trail from Ottawa to Vancouver, then Arizona, and finally, Vienna. Her details checked out. And in 1997, my epic 12,000-word feature about Frannie and the scab of shame she was picking off her family's hidden history ran in the *Ottawa Citizen* newspaper. The story was called "Our Father," subtitled: "The roots of fear: Frances Sheridan's play, The Waltonsteins, forced her family to confront the demons of its secret past."

The story focused on Frannie's quest to expose a truth her father had long kept hidden: he wasn't actually Dr. Bernie Sheridan, a well-known Ottawa eye doctor. He was Dr. Bernie Sigal, a Holocaust survivor who had hidden his identity from his seven children and instead raised them as Catholic, sending them to a religious school and mass on Sundays. The consequences to the mental health of his family were profound. Like many children of Holocaust survivors, who sort through their pain and confusion through the arts — theatre, writing, art, stand-up comedy —Frannie, the second youngest, eventually started performing comedy as catharsis. By revealing her truth to strangers, she tried to heal the second-generational trauma, even though she didn't yet think of herself as a Jew.

Meeting Frannie for the first time in Vancouver (she now lives in Florida), I found her funny, scattered, nonlinear, and inspirational. She is a seeker and truth teller. Yet, teasing out a straightforward narrative of her childhood was impossible, making me sometimes doubt her story, revealed in acts and anecdotes fit for a stage. I craved a chronological narrative fit for a Protestant and demanded documentation, which she supplied. Afterward, I flew to Arizona to confirm details with one of her sisters, then flew to Vienna to meet Dr. Sheridan. His family was shocked that he agreed to the interview, but he told me he wanted people to understand his journey and sympathize with his choices. "Make sure in your story you talk about that Madeleine Albright woman," he said, referring to the U.S. Secretary of State, who had announced that same year, 1997, that she'd only recently found out that her Jewish parents had fled Czechoslovakia before the war and converted to Catholicism, hiding their true identities in America.

On a cool Thursday morning, I met the former Dr. Sigal in the courtyard of the Josephinium, once part of the medical college of the University of Vienna, where he had studied medicine.

> *A small man wearing the yellow armband of the blind, sits on a bench in the courtyard, arms resting on his white cane. Abruptly he throws down his cane and holds up trembling hands. "His arms, they were this big. He must have been a mechanic or a butcher," he says. "He wore brass knuckles."*
>
> *This is the building where Bernie Sigal was attacked by a Nazi 61 years ago. This is where Dr. Bernie Sheridan weeps today.*
>
> *"It's endless. Endless," the 84-year-old said of grief so fresh it's as if the attack came yesterday.*
>
> *He talked in detail about his life as Bernie Sigal, in Vienna, France and even Saskatchewan. But his life as Dr. Bernie Sheridan in Ottawa was unreachable.*

I interviewed Dr. Sheridan for several days and on some, he talked of his duplicitous life with regret. "When you want to protect your children you will do anything. Maybe, I went too far," he said. On other days, he said defiantly, "I would do it all over again." Then, an hour later, he'd claim none of it had happened and he was a perfect father to his happy, well-adjusted children. Shuffling down the street, white cane clicking against grey stones, he asked, "What do children really know about their parents? What are parents supposed to tell their children? Everything? Do you terrify them? What do you do?"

When "Our Father" was published in the *Ottawa Citizen*, it moved and astonished many people in Ottawa, including those who had gone to school with the Sheridan children or were patients of Dr. Sheridan. A Jewish synagogue and a Catholic parish came together to bring Frannie to Ottawa to perform her one-woman play to a standing ovation. That connection still exists today as Team Waltonstein. On that weekend, many of her estranged family members also came to see her perform, some who never forgave her for revealing family secrets and betraying their privacy.

I played a small part in connecting Frannie with the famed Hollywood director Arthur Hiller, who died in 2016. He flew to meet her after having read my article and offered to help share her story with the world. The movie they envisioned is still yet to be made, but in your hands, you hold Frannie's memoir, which has taken more than two decades to write, and was a lifetime in the making. I think because it holds so many uncomfortable truths and asks so many difficult questions she struggled to find a publisher, until now.

Frannie's story is unconventional and uncompromising in ways that make even me feel uncomfortable, prudish. Only by reading her book did I come to understand the contradictory fear and fear-lessness that dominates her life; so afraid to raise her voice, but more so to remain silent. She'd been raised to believe that if she told anyone she was Jewish she would be risking her life — and her family's — because many hidden Nazis and anti-Semites were just waiting for an opportunity to eliminate Jews, or so her father told her. As she pushed against her father's boundaries, he threatened her with institutionalization in a mental hospital.

After I met her, after she had performed her play for years and had the support of the renowned Hiller, she actually became a stripper for a short while to make peace with elements of her past, and herself. How could becoming a stripper help a second-generation Holocaust survivor? I see now that her choice to strip was a way to confront a lingering layer of crippling shame leftover from her father's emotional abuse and subsequent sexual abuse she suffered at the hands of others. Also, it's perversely funny: an utterly naked Frannie standing mocking the male clientele in a strip club made her feel powerful and free.

Frannie's story celebrates the resilience of the human spirit. As she says, she's "come out of the wormhole with joy and humour" and now broadcasts a daily playful, uplifting hour-long livestream called Facebook Love to a global audience.

My dear friend of so many years is impossible to put down. So is her book. And that's no joke.

Shelley Page
Ottawa, 2021

Prologue

As I stepped onstage half-naked in my see-through, sparkly gold cover-up at a small strip club in a backwater town near the Washington State border, I heard one of the regulars, a hard-drinking biker guy shout, "Take it off, baby. Take it all off." That's all I needed to hear. I hungered to perform and to really be seen. I had spent far too long hiding who I was. Luckily, I had my mother's genes: at thirty-nine I was still hot. I had strong dancer's legs, curves in all the right places and boobs that looked you straight in the eye.

While gyrating my hips I thought, "This should remove the last layer of crap! Along with my clothes I'll finally cast off that horrible feeling that something is wrong with me. Raised to believe I was Catholic when I was actually Jewish, I grew up thinking that sharing truths about myself could get me killed or worse – locked up in a mental institution. There had to be something deeply wrong with me. Why else would people want to kill or incarcerate me if they found out who I really was?

Still, I had gone ahead and revealed my Jewish identity onstage by performing a one-woman show. Yet even with that disclosure, something was barring me from feeling free. I sensed that the way out was to expose another shame-based aspect of myself.

One of the most forbidden acts for a nice Jewish girl is to bare it all for strangers. Jewish girls are taught the Prime Directive at a very early age, long before learning how to cook, sew, or obtain more credit cards after maxing out the ones they have. The Prime Directive is very simple – you cannot expose your body to strangers if you hope to get a "good Jewish husband," such as a doctor, an attorney or even some schlemiel with wealthy parents.

There are two exceptions to the Prime Directive: (A) If you are a famous Jewish actress (i.e. Scarlett Johansson), you can expose it all on the wide screen for fifty million people, including simulated sex. No big deal. Any Jewish male with half a brain will still be thrilled to marry you for the pleasure of witnessing his friends' twisted expressions scream: *You can get a piece of that whenever you want, and I'll never be able to!* (B) If you aren't Jewish, it doesn't matter if you've been gracing the pole for ten years, as long as you're now retired. You automatically fall into the Trophy Wife category, which is always acceptable.

Other than working as a "peeler" in a gentleman's club, pretty much everything else is acceptable behavior for Jewish females. You can treat your employees like cattle, cheat the tax man and even go to jail. All of that's fine. Just ask Leona Helmsley, the daughter of Polish-Jewish immigrants and gold-digging wife of hotel magnate Harry Helmsley who ruled her empire like the Queen of Hearts. When she got out of prison, Harry and the rest of society were waiting for her with open arms. Likewise, Marilyn Monroe, who converted to Judaism in the '50s and bared it all for the readers of *Playboy*. Still, Arthur Miller, America's greatest Jewish playwright, was thrilled to marry her. But poor misguided Monica Lewinsky, who was raised Jewish, the granddaughter of Lithuanian and Russian grandparents bowed to our President and was sentenced to disgrace for the rest of her life. Rules are rules.

And as for the Laws of Gravity, most Jewish girls are academically accomplished, so they understand that once they pass the age of thirty, what used to stand proudly and stare at the ceiling now looks at the floor.

Okay, full disclosure: you may not know where or when you've seen me, but it's very likely that you have. In addition to performing live stage plays, some which won mayoral awards in Florida, and being in demand as a Restaurant Dessert Reviewer (having inherited the Jewish cheesecake gene I'm a natural at over-eating dessert!) I have been sought after as a Humorist and Stress Management Speaker, sharing techniques to better navigate Shame, Fear and Guilt. So, you're probably wondering "What's a nice Jewish girl doing taking her clothes off in public?" Well, as they say, "we teach what we need to learn." And to manage my stress, I needed to take off my clothes.

Shame, Fear, and Guilt continued to haunt me long after I was extolled for my professional contributions. Being a second-generation child of Holocaust survivors came with emotional weight. The war may have ended in Europe, but it's long-reaching fingers continued to battle within many descendants. Some of us are understandably pretty screwed up. In my case, exhausted by the hypocrisy I felt in teaching methods to combat emotional strain while internally imploding much of the time, as well as the duplicity which I observed outside of myself left me feeling ashamed and angry. But being my strong survivor parent's daughter, I was determined to win over my inner Nazi.

Like a juicy Long Island mosquito to a bug light, I was magnetized to what made me feel shame. But what did I have to be ashamed of? After all my plays were backed by Canadian congressional Senators, who gave me a tour of the capitol as an honored guest. Documentaries about my work were produced, one was even awarded the Gabriel (for excellence in broadcasting). My standup comedy act was broadcast internationally. I'd been in cable TV movies and, in all likelihood, by the time the book is published, network television. I'd been blessed to be a protégé of Arthur Hiller, famed director of *Love Story*, and I'd appeared with Sid Caeser, Keanu Reeves, Mark Breslin and Seth Rogen. I would point out they were very nice to me. (I've omitted mentioning the assholes.)

As strange as it sounds with all of this goodness in tow, I felt the need to more deeply heal myself and further bare my soul by shedding any remaining inhibitions. So, there I was, on my very first day working as an exotic dancer.

Chapter 1

I pulled on my long red wig, grabbed my CD's and fake fur blanket, and loped down the stairs in the super-high stripper sandals I had almost learned to walk in. On the landing, I took a moment and gazed around the beer-scented gentleman's club. Two twenty-something strippers chatted a few feet away, their backs to me. Although I only caught glimpses of their tight-skinned necks, faces and legs, it was sufficient to torture me with imagined images of their perfectly alluring young bodies. I gulped, remembering the bloat I'd begun to see on myself. Just then, one of the gals turned and looked at me. She waved and smiled exposing a tooth gap. She was stunning. A young Lauren Hutton, the toothy supermodel of the '70s and '80s. I tensed my neck. At least it felt tight. I forced a smile. She walked away as the other young woman ambled over; an unsmiling fine-boned brunette with huge blue eyes who wore glasses which made her ridiculously irresistible. I was relieved to feel more maternal than jealous. My regime of meditation, visualizations, and affirmations was paying off – Maybe I'd reach nirvana one of these days.

She extended a hand. "Haven't seen you before. I'm Doctor Boobra Streisand." Before I could respond, she continued, "Well, the doctor parts real anyway. Just completed my PhD in Women's Studies."

Just as I uttered "Wow!" she shrugged "Paying off my bigass student loan. You?" She cocked her head at me, waiting.

She was correct, I needed money too. But the last thing I was going to do was admit this to pre-pubescent Madonna. I gave her a thumbs-up.

Barely noticing, she continued, "I hope you take this the way I intend it, but I think the fact you're middle-aged and doing this is super brave!"

My skin flushed with shame. It took me a second to recover. My experience handling hecklers in the audience while working as a stand-up comedian weighed in.

Using the British accent I'd practiced, I puffed out my chest and intoned breathily, "Oh yes, pumpkin. I am indeed. That is, if by middle-aged you mean well-seasoned and juicy!" I patted my hair a la Mae West.

She laughed conspiratorially. "You work it, girlfriend!" She did a little twist causing the flap on her wrap-around robe to open uncovering her lack of a muffin top, I felt my eyes widen. She saw and smiled. Damn! I took consolation in telling myself that she could be my daughter whose firm tummy I would be thrilled about.

The crowd was buzzing. She turned to scour the room as I flexed my thighs. I was getting a little puffy in places, but my legs were still firm, cellulite and all. Years of dance training had come in handy.

She laughed, then looked back at me. "Alcohol makes them so cocky. They think they're dating us!"

"Bloody hell!" I purred like Dame Maggie Smith. "But the fab thing is booze helps to make vision a tad blurry so that my cottage cheese thighs aren't quite as irresistible…don't want to have to hire a silly bodyguard!"

Her expression didn't shift. My irony hadn't resonated with her cellulite-free self.

"Love your accent!" she quipped at me.

A muscular young man wearing coveralls slammed his work belt on the counter of the bar. He looked up at her and smiled. They made silent goo-goo eyes at each other. "Get over here, Dr. Boobra, my dick's exploding!" he roared playfully. "I need a prostate exam and I need it now!"

"Then again, there is the exception to every rule," she said to me, giggling as she glided over to him.

Their chemistry was magnetic. I knew I should stop staring. I closed my eyes and envisioned a halo of protective energy surrounding me to keep out whatever weirdness I might encounter from the hungry men in the audience. Still standing on the landing of the stairs, I turned to hold on to the banister, placed one leg on the wall, and stretched. Hearing something crunch under the sole of my shoe, I took my leg down, then turned the foot over to check. "Uch!" I peeled the cockroach cadaver off my shoe with the edge of the CD case. "Yuck!"

For a moment I yearned for the upscale theater located close to the city of my birth – Ottawa, where I'd recently performed a solo play. In that play I revealed some of the secrets my parents had so ardently guarded about my religious identity. Although sharing that aspect of my family story had given me a forum to uncover a few of the hidden pieces of myself, I was terrified about exposing more personal ones. I wrestled with emotional paralysis in many areas of my life, having recently extricated myself from a seven-year relationship with an extremely jealous boyfriend.

"Why did you look at him, Frannie? Now he's looking at you!" was a common jeer. Then he'd rigidly walk up to the unsuspecting guy and say, "What the fuck are you looking at?"

His puffed-up testosterone had garnered him many a black eye. The anxiety had felt all too familiar, and thus I had initially fallen easily under his crazy spell. I wanted to make sure that phase was over.

Driven to be onstage as an actress and comic, I was compelled to find a way to rid myself of more layers of fear so that I could be my naked self in the public eye, and not care about the evaluation. Although I had some success with comedy having performed an irreverent feminist standup comedy show across the country, and toured with a headliner as his opening act, I still battled occasional tsunami-sized waves of terror which made regular stage fright look like kids play. When bookings were slim, to make money I decided to work as a stripper. Although I had never been to a gentleman's club prior to my audition for work as a professional peeler, once I was hired, I was unstoppable.

Exposing sides of myself that had been previously considered taboo had served me well in the past. I still had layers to shed before I stopped caring how others saw me. Working as an exotic dancer felt like the next best step.

I called myself *SmartiePanties*.

In perfecting my new role as a professional sexy person, I would be leaving very little to the imagination.

The end of Van Halen's song "Poundcake" blared from the speakers, as catcalls were directed at the six-foot-tall stripper, *Cherry Pie*. I squinted at her through the smoky air. Smiling, she closed her robe. My stomach clenched. I was moments away from being up there in the buff.

I peered out at the customers, hoping not to recognize anyone, hoping not to be identified. Although the peeler club was eight hours from my home in Vancouver, my fear was not unjustified. I had taken a bus and gotten chatty with the person who sat next to me. Turned out he'd seen my play. Thankfully, he assumed that I was en route to perform at a legitimate theater. I didn't deny it and rode the rest of the way to my first stripping gig in uncomfortable silence, praying that I would be far enough from home to escape any further enquiry – at least by anybody I knew personally.

I thought that I was home free…until the bus stopped in front of a nondescript looking building, save for the address. Although it was unsettling that the club appeared to be intentionally somewhat hidden from street view, I was relieved it wasn't sporting a huge neon sign that said something like "Welcome to the Bouncy Lemons Gentleman's Club". I had forgotten that I'd asked the driver to drop me off. Luckily my companion was engaged in reading. I bit my tongue. *Don't look up, don't look up!* He looked up.

"You're getting off here? It's a strip bar. Rough neighborhood. Someone coming to meet you?" I held my breath. Recognizing my discomfort, he pretended to return to his book. I hastily lifted my over-sized suitcase down and dragged it down the aisle.

Once on the sidewalk, I shivered in my parka. The frosty air caused me to cough. He knocked on the window. I waved quickly, pretended to check my watch, then glanced across the street as if waiting for someone. He mouthed "Are you okay?" I gave a thumbs-up, then rechecked my watch as the bus drove away.

Now, inside the showroom, I was soothed by a familiar sensation. My crotch had moistened, and my face was flushed. Panic had been replaced by titillation. Sharing hidden parts of myself in public as a playwright, and now as a stripper, turned me on. I had spent far too much of my life pretending.

Chapter 2

Until I was nine years old, I thought our family, the Sheridans, were Irish-Catholic. Dad had told me we were "related to St. Patrick himself," and I believed him. Why wouldn't I? I still believed in the Tooth Fairy. Plus, he was only five foot two inches, way shorter than all the other dads, which I figured was a result of his leprechaun blood. And if that hadn't been proof enough, Mother bought corned beef when it was on sale; and cooked it for us together with what I thought was her European recipe for potato pancakes. Also, we attended St. Basil's church every Sunday.

Religiously.

At eight, I was perched to be confirmed by Father O'Malley, who had told me "The custom of confirmation means that you are marrying Jesus." My first response was to feel trapped by the idea of an arranged marriage, and I wondered if Jesus looked anything like Donny Osmond. Then I thought about whether Jesus was an eye surgeon like dad.

At the time, it took me a minute to realize that Father O'Malley had meant it figuratively. Back then, I took everything literally.

Walking into church and seeing the candles lit near the altar always felt like a special occasion. I loved going to confession because, as far as I was concerned, it was the best of two worlds; I got to talk, and the priest was forced to listen.

Years later, my ex-husband would refer to that dynamic as having been the main problem in our marriage.

But as a little girl, I loved it. My mom was generally too busy or exhausted to listen to me, and dad worked all the time. I called him Diddy because he had told me that was how to pronounce the word

Daddy. When I did that, it seemed to please him so I didn't question him, even though I had a feeling that it had to do with the fact that he had told me that he learned English as a second language.

When we were in church I also loved participating in rituals such as genuflecting before sitting in a pew or at the altar, as well as saying prayers and singing hymns. Knowing what to do and say next made me feel smart. Plus, we rarely had guests over to our home, but at church it felt like us Sheridans were included as part of a larger family.

Even though the communion wafer wasn't exactly a snack, it seemed like one. But, I had a couple of problems with it; like the priest touching the wafer, and then placing it on people's tongues'. Yuck, it should have been covered in Saran Wrap. Why we couldn't just pick it up ourselves never made sense to me. Or he could have just passed out toothpicks, I thought.

Although communion made me hungry, I knew that we would be having yummy egg rolls later at The Golden Palace, the Chinese food restaurant where we ate every Sunday, or had take-out. The owner was one of Dad's patients. On the way out, my dad would bow and thank him for the meal, which he usually gave us for free; Doh je, he would say in Cantonese. He told me he had learned how during a trip for a meeting with other eye surgeons to what was then called the Orient. The owner of the Chinese restaurant would sweetly reply, "You're welcome." and bow in return. Then Dad would copy his accent. "You Weh-com, weh-com!" he would repeat rapidly. Although it was a bang-on imitation, neither the owner or anyone in his family ever smiled in response, which made me gnaw the inside of my mouth. I could tell that Dad's behavior was wrong although I didn't know why and I knew that saying anything to him would only cause more problems.

In some ways, church felt like a magical world. It was one of the rare places where Mother allowed me to wear a fancy dress. I thought it was because the priests wore dresses too. I loved it when they sang and spoke in Latin, even though I couldn't understand. It made me feel as if my family and I were members of a secret club.

One Sunday, a baby was baptized. Hearing the infant cry made me cringe.

Dad noticed. "Only small drops of water," he said, rubbing my arm.

I made eye contact with Mom, but she looked away.

I didn't question the way the world was presented.

Chapter 3

I was nine years old. Someone was whispering my name. "Frances! Frances!"

"Wha-what time is it? Are you okay?" I mumbled towards the dark figure standing over my bed.

He moved within the glow of the Raggedy Ann nightlight. Even though the air was cold, his forehead shone from sweat. "Come quickly and meet me in the empty room!"

I didn't think not to do what he said. He was my dad. As the sixth of seven children, I could never get enough of his attention. I wished that there was a way for me to squish him into my heart, so that I could always keep him with me.

I untangled myself from my cocoon of blankets and shivered in the December air. Ottawa had earned the title "the cold city" for good reason. Still, Mother insisted we keep the thermostat at what Dad called a Siberian level. Nothing was to be indulged because that was considered wasteful.

I burrowed into my housecoat, which was about as warming as I imagined the onionskin paper Diddy wrote letters on, but I was eager to hear what he had to say. He had never disturbed me in the night before.

He had moved into the shadows, and I could barely see him. It felt creepy. I shuddered. But I slumped across the hall and followed him into the bedroom that had belonged to my twin sisters until they moved into the university dormitories. Diddy had a desk light on in the far corner of the room. He stood there, lit up by the glare, using a corner of his vertically striped blue and white nightshirt, to clean his glasses.

"Important that everything is well in focus!" he muttered without looking up. "Close the door quietly and sit."

He waited until I was seated on one of the desk chairs, then looked at me for a good minute, as if in a daze.

"This is very important Frances. You remember, I started to tell you at lunch today? But it was not the time nor the place to go into detail. Do not interrupt! You are nine now. Old enough to know."

His Adams apple changed position a few times.

Diddy loved to lecture me about things like the importance of getting good grades and why misbehaving would lead me down a path to hell. So I knew he expected my complete attention. I sat up very straight. He didn't appreciate my slouching.

He smiled. "Good girl. Jah, 1951, we lived in the Midwest. Saskatchewan. A decade or so before you were born. A small Prairie town called Morse – I had my first medical practice there."

I knew that my parents and four oldest siblings had lived in a small town before I was born, but they hardly spoke about it so I hadn't really thought about it. But what he said next was news to me.

"This followed redoing my degree. You see, Frances, I fled Vienna without papers. Medical credentials."

I nodded to let him know I understood, even though this was the first I'd heard about fleeing Vienna and I had no idea what medical credentials were. Both my parents were European, which was why they spoke broken English with accents, and my mom cooked some food I figured she'd eaten when she was little. Matzo ball soup, and liverwurst, and every spring those triangle-shaped cookies filled with jam. She bought egg-flavored matzos all year round, which I assumed were over-sized European crackers.

Diddy smiled. "Jah, so, the twins were already little girls. And Philip was one. Martha was growing in your Momma's belly, and I made enough." He came over and stood right in front of me. "Now listen, Frances. At that time, your mother and I were still observant Jews." He cleared his throat, looked towards the door, and then continued in a quiet voice. "Jewish is a culture, a religion. Observant means strict. It's what we were." He swallowed and, from his expression, it looked like a piece of hard candy going down. "This is a secret to tell no one, Frances! No one!"

I scrunched my toes so hard they began to cramp. He waited for me to nod.

"But it was impossible. We were Orthodox! Oodles of rituals, Frances. Only eating certain foods, and so on." He shrugged. "We were the only Jews in the little *ferkukta* – crappy town. We felt like aliens. Sunday, church bells rang nonstop. Everyone who lived there walked past our home on the way to church."

I kept my eyes on Diddy, trying to understand what he was saying and to keep my posture straight. I attended a Catholic school and some of the teachers were nuns. On Sundays, when the church bells rang, Dad took us to church. My sisters and I had worn flowing white dresses to our Confirmation ceremonies.

"When we lived out there in the Midwest, the nearest kosher store was hundreds of miles away," Diddy continued. I was about to ask what kosher was, but he said, "Kosher, Frances, are customs, traditions. That Jewish people keep."

I nodded, not really understanding but wanting to convince him to continue. Being asked to listen to my dad's middle-of-the night lecture made me feel ultra-important. He'd said I was old enough now to know the truth. I didn't want him to think I wasn't mature.

Diddy nodded to himself in silence. He ran his fingers through sweaty strands of his thinning, salt and pepper hair. He told me an anti-Semite was "someone who hated Jewish people." Anti-Semites feel threatened by Jews, he explained, and even in so-called beautiful North America this insanity persisted. According to my dad, many European-Christians lived in the small Midwestern town and they had "spread old anti-Semitic lies like a contagious disease."

He came closer to me. "You see, the townspeople would point, and whisper, and so forth, but your Mother and I didn't think we were in any outright danger. Didn't think, jah. But one day, Peter Schmidt barges into my office. A doctor, can you imagine? With his wife. And began to beat me. My patient ran out. Schmidt and his wife threatened to 'make my family into dog food'."

Diddy stared at me. His eyes were watery. He shook his head and gulped some air, trying to calm down. "I couldn't go on living, if anything ever happened to you and the others!" He pulled his mouth into an ugly smirk, like he was staring down an invisible enemy. "I spat at him. Felt a searing pain. Heard a crack.

He had used a small alabaster bust of Freud I had sitting on my desk to try to smash my skull."

No, no, no! How dare he hurt my Diddy!

I leapt up to hug him. "Diddy, Diddy." I fastened myself to him as if together we could become one thicker skin. He peeled my hands from his belly and held both of them in his for a moment. "Sweetheart, Diddy's okay. I just tell you these things to protect you. Sit, and I'll finish."

Until then, I hadn't noticed that a patch of light shining on the curtain from the streetlamp turned it the yellow-green color of puke.

"I heard police sirens. I came to. I had been unconscious, Frances. I couldn't see well. Felt for my glasses. Fractured lenses. I was lying in a pool of dark moisture. I saw it was my blood." He looked down at the ground with disgust, then at the wall. "Those pigs had written graffiti on the walls..." Diddy became frantic, and shouted, "Of my office! In my own blood!" He nodded towards the walls of the room we were in. *"Christ Killers*! Other bad words, Frances, you shouldn't have to know!"

He must have noticed my lost expression. "The same old story. They're always accusing us of killing Jesus Christ. You remember the story with Pontius Pilate, and so forth? From your Catechism studies?"

I nodded. And at that very moment I made the connection. We were Jews. The Jews I'd learned about in Catechism class, the people who killed Jesus were our ancestors. And the people who had beaten Diddy were Christian.

I chewed the nail of my already chewed pinky until it hurt like heck.

Diddy sharply sucked in air. "The Schmidts were fined a paltry thirty dollars. For assault. They thought it was a joke at that court-house. Some judge, the honorable Thomson! Judge, my *tuchas* – bottom. In the end he will be judged correctly, by the Maker. Jew-haters are always hiding in dark holes, Frances. Like cockroaches. Just waiting for the right moment to emerge. So, we left that hellhole. I changed our family name from Sigal, which is Jewish, Frances, to Sheridan."

I had a different last name?

He went on. "Many people hate Jews and would happily kill you, and our whole family. So we are Catholic! That is what you tell people. Nothing else. Ever! Never, ever let down your guard. And not a peep to anyone in the family until I clarify who is and who isn't on our side…too much for one day. I will tell you more another time. But Frances, you simply can't trust anyone but me. But I will always be here for you. We will take care of each other. I tell you Frances, another Holocaust is always just around the corner! But not a peep to anyone, I mean *anyone*. You understand Frances?"

"I understand," I said.

Dad's decision to hide who we were made sense to me. I appreciated that he was trying to protect us. We were Catholic, and that was good. We were Jewish, and that was dangerous.

But it felt like something cold was sucking at my heart. What about all the Catholic people I'd thought we belonged with? Were they our friends? And what exactly was a Holocaust?

I was too wiped out to ask for explanations. Diddy seemed to have run out of words He yawned and patted my shoulder. "Okay sweet girl, I have to perform cataract surgery in the a. m. I don't want to give anybody a third eye!" He chuckled to himself, then realizing I didn't get his joke, he waved the air away. "Jah, so go back to bed now. You have school in the morning."

He kissed me on the forehead, opened the door to the hallway, and walked towards his bedroom.

My younger brother was still sound asleep when I returned to my room. I crawled back into my woolen igloo of blankets, but I couldn't sleep. I lay there for hours, wide-eyed, thinking about the things I'd just learned, reminding myself to always keep our family story a Fort Knox level secret.

Little did I know that I would spend the rest of my life dealing with the consequences.

Case File 2016-572
Dear Frannie Sheridan:

Thank you for your phone call of April 21st concerning the assault on your father Bernie Sigal. The case was heard by Magistrate G.C. Thomson of Swift Current but in the town of Herbert some distance to the East. I have located the newspaper article from the Regina *Leader-Post*. I have also found a slightly longer article in the April 25th, 1951 issue of the Swift Current newspaper *The Sun*. It says that the accused, Dr. Peter P.H. Schmidt and his wife made the assault on Dr. Bernard Sigal [sic] while he was in the act of examining a patient. Dr. Sigal suffered some concussion in the assault. He was represented by J.E. Friesen of Swift Current.

Sincerely,
Tim Novak
Reference Archivist
Reference Services Unit
Provincial Archives of Saskatchewan
P.O. Box 1665
Regina SK S4P 3C6
Phone: 306-787-4068
Fax: 306-787-1197
Email: info.regina@archives.gov.sk.ca
Website: www.saskarchives.com

Frannie Sheridan is looking for a court record involving her father Bernie Sigal. He was a doctor in Morse, Saskatchewan and was assaulted in 1951. There is an article about the case in the Leader Post from April 21st, 1951, pg. 2 titled "Doctor Fined." The AMICUS number is 7614349 and the case concluded with a fine for Dr. and Mrs. Schmidt.

Saturday, April 21, 1951

Doctor fined

MORSE, Sask., (Special).—Dr. P. P. Schmidt, Herbert, pleaded guilty to a charge of common assault against Dr. B. Segal, Morse, April 17, and was fined $20 and costs by Magistrate G. C. Thomson, K.C., of Swift Current. Mrs. Schmidt was fined $10 for aiding and abetting her husband in the assault.

Chapter 4

Thirty years later, back at the strip bar, I stood in the dingy showroom shivering in my skimpy gold glitter costume. Even though I wore a cocky little smile and my nipples had become pert, my heart had begun to beat so hard I could hear it in my ears.

"I am protected by layers of love", I repeated to myself although even I didn't buy it.

What if one of the theatrical producers who had booked an upcoming performance of the play I'd written about embracing my religious identity was out there? These were people for whom pious beliefs were central, but I'd heard that some devout men and women secretly frequent sexual establishments. Could the unveiling of our covert identities result in their terminating my play contract? I was very enthusiastic about my upcoming theatrical engagements, intending to use my downtime to draw out more memories and write additional scenes for the play.

Straightening my back, I strutted to the bar holding my head high. I coughed, hoping the smoky air would help camouflage me. Feeling the intensity of the crowds gaze elevated my mood. My skin suddenly felt electric. The thought of controlling spectators by doing a forbidden sexual dance made me tingle.

A few of the rough-'n'-tough patrons were hovering around the stage waiting to be sexed-up by my routine, eyes rolling over me like stoned teenagers about to devour a cheesy hot pizza. The bald, beefy bartender looked up at me from where he was crouched in front of the open fridge doing his beer bottle count.

"You the first dancer?" he grunted.

"Indeed, love," I crooned in my phony British accent.

He squinted, poker-faced. I tried not to move and maintained eye contact. Did he think I was faking it? Remembering that my Brighton-based friend, Diana, had validated the authenticity of my elocution, I relaxed a little. "My name's SmartiePanties. What's yours?"

His bulging eyes protruded. "Smiley."

Bathed in the green light from the refrigerator icemaker, he looked like Kermit the Frog on meth.

"SmartiePanties? Really? Fuck off!"

"Fucking A!" I replied without flinching. Breathe, just breathe.

"SmartiePanties," he repeated with a tiny smirk. He pointed to the sound system. "You're responsible for your own music. Full show's eighteen minutes. Half show's ten. Anything less, fifty-dollar fine. Missed show's a hundred. More than two missed, you're out. If you're late, you're out. No physical contact, no drinks while you're dancing. Be ready to go on five minutes before your show. Any paint shows, water shows, soap shows are your responsibility to clean up. No G-string tipping, tips on the stage only. Get your shit together, your show starts in two minutes or you're late."

"Got it lovie" I said, spreading my mouth into a talk-show-host grin.

He turned away. I exhaled, then silently mouthed "Bite me, Smiley!"

I grimaced, then called to him. "One more *eensy* thing Smiley; could I trouble you for a glass of ice, love ducky?"

I went over to the CD player and geared up my music selection. *What If God Was One Of Us* by Joan Osborne, began to play. A quick glance around the room convinced me that if God was really one of us, we were royally fucked.

Smiley shoved a glass of ice at me. "Bust a cherry, sweetheart!"

"Thank you, muffin." I scanned the packed room for a moment. It caused the vein in my neck to pulsate. *You know what you're doing this for, you know what you're doing this for*, went my inner chant, as I headed for the stage. I threw myself into a wild boogie to conceal my splintering nerves. As I drew close, I noticed that the stage was lined with potted poinsettia plants adorned with silver tinsel. *Oy, it's Christmas Eve*, I mused, climbing the stairs on all fours. I thought about Betsey, the pet cat we had when we were children. She had walked through the house trailing silver tinsel from her rear end.

An intoxicated man, well over ninety years old, gurgled, "Whad the fug is this shit music?" I placed my glass of ice on the floor and faced my critic.

"Well, Fa la la Tootsie!" I said, shimming for him for a few seconds.

"She's British!" yelped a stringy-haired, fifty-something man leaning against the stage. "Say something else!"

The bartender announced my entrance. "Our first dancer of the day is all the way from England, he-e-ere's SmartiePanties!" The men whistled and clapped. I picked up one of the plants and teased the boys by holding it in front of my private parts.

"Do you like my bush, fellas?" I inquired, winking at my adoring aged admirer.

"Tha-a-a's the only kinn'a bush you'll see in these parts any-more, eh baby!" he drooled at me.

A drunk fireman said, "Peelers don' normally dance to God songs, baby! You raisin' money to become a nun?" His buddies laughed along with him.

"Amen, Tootsie!" I began to boogie around the stage flaunting my behind, which is one of my finest assets. I placed the plant back down on the stage, stroking its petals.

I could hear people greeting Smiley as well as each other and realized that the bar was filling up with regulars. Mostly tough-looking men some with girlfriends and wives, hookers, plus a cop sporting an enormous mustache, pretending to be working, pink-faced from the cold rain. Employing a slapstick move, I fake walked into the pole and tumbled backwards, causing a few guffaws. A patron snarled, "Lucille Ball go home!" Animal-like, I crawled up the pole, then swung onto it, hugging it inside my legs. I propelled my body around a few times, and then stopped with the strength of my inner thighs. Letting go of the pole to allow for a back arch, I opened my hands wide. My robe dropped to the ground. I was wearing a mini skirt with a Velcro enclosure. My back stretch caused it to slowly open, then fall off. Delighted yelps from the audience. Then silence. I had sewn a bright pink udder onto my underwear, hoping it would get a laugh. It didn't.

"What, is this s'posed to be some kinda fuckin' joke?" the same man bellowed.

I felt the blood beating in my ears, and flashed on a memory of the time my dad had purchased a quirky knickknack at The Joke Shop which had a similar impact.

Chapter 5

When I was nine years old, dad bought a silly toy called "The Laughing Bag" from The Joke Shop. You pressed a button which made laughing sounds come from inside a small orange sack. At first, I loved how much fun it was. But then, Diddy began to use the Laughing Bag to force us kids to cheer up. Sometimes, after one of his everyday arguments with mom, which also upset us, he'd start the bag. You'd hear a tinny "Yuk, yuk, yuk!"

Then dad would demand, "Now everybody repeat, "Yuk, yuk yuk!" We gloomily chanted, "Yuk, yuk, yuk".

I liked the idea of it but hated that it always backfired. The more often Diddy got us to repeat the words the worse we sounded. It made my gut clamp. I was always worried he was going to snap. During yuk yuk sessions, I pulled on strands of my hair 'till it hurt to give myself something else to think about.

Decades later, I shared this experience with a comedy club crowd and it was heartwarming hearing their laughter. It made me feel a little less like a weirdo.

Comedy Club Palm Beach 2018

What a fun audience – any parents here? Kids are so expensive, aren't they? But I've decided it's time. So I'm adopting a fifty year old Harvard graduate to support me! Hey, ya gotta get your breaks where you can – it's a tough job. My Dad could've used more fun being a parent– he was Austrian and super regimented and serious butcha' know Austrians and Germans aren't known for their sense of humor.

Like you never hear of a chain of comedy clubs called 'Himmler's Ha-ha Huts'! But my Dad deserves credit for trying - he bought this toy called a Laughing Bag which emits canned laughter when you squeeze it. He obviously hoped that it would help break the tension at home - but he'd bring it out at the most inappropriate times! Like after a funeral! Okay, it was for our cat but still... we were upset. And if you force laughter when you're troubled it sounds scary. He was like (German accent) "Repeat hahaha after za bag! Shnell!" So we'd go (angry) "HAAA HAAA HAAA!" It sounded like an ISIS rally at a beheading!

Chapter 6

Catching myself giggling out loud while reading 'The Cat In The Hat' made me laugh even more. But then, the salty-fatty smell of Mom's cooking floated upstairs.

"All Sheridans to the dining room immediately!" she called in her sing-songy voice, then rang the dinner bell.

I dog-eared a page from my Dr. Seuss book and practically bounced down the stairs, making the long rosary chain – a present from Sister Mary Therese – dance on my chest. While rubbing the square corners of the tiny crucifix pendant, I remembered some of the scary things Diddy had shared with me. I wondered whether the nun would make me return the necklace to her if she found out that I was Jewish? I hoped not, even though I had figured out that it wasn't made in the Holy Land when I saw the sticker on the back which read 'Made in China'.

Mom laughed strangely when she saw me wearing it earlier that day, but I loved wearing over-sized jewelry. I thought maybe it had something to do with what Diddy told me, but I was too pooped from school to say something about it.

Even though everyone was already gathered, Mother, wearing the blue-print house dress which she wore on special occasions like full family dinners when everyone comes, continued to shake the bronze bell until I arrived. I plunked down at the vinyl cloth-covered table with Diddy and my brothers and sisters, wishing Momma had used the prettier lace tablecloth which made dinner time feel just a little special. At least she had laid out linen napkins. I spread mine on my lap and gulped the bowl of steaming matzo-ball soup set before me. Then it hit me and my heart raced. *Was the food we were eating really*

Jewish? Dad had said there was something called kosher food that Jewish people ate. I thought my parents were European and then found out they were Jewish. I thought matzo-ball soup was a German European chicken dumpling soup. Maybe it was also kosher food?

I watched mom sigh, then retreat into the kitchen to sit alone as usual. Feeling her sadness always made me feel tired. I'd given up asking why she didn't sit with us in the dining room for meals. She mostly shrugged or else said "Frances, this is just easier," as if she wanted me to believe that being closer to the refrigerator and stove somehow made it easier for her to get to the dining room table. I didn't push it with my question because I knew that I would just upset her. I didn't understand all of the reasons, but I knew it was because of the secret Diddy shared with me.

I nibbled from the bowl of pork rinds he liked to eat at the dinner table (to annoy mom). While wondering if the pork rinds had something to do with being Jewish, I tried my best to hear what he was whispering to my eldest sister, Sally. *Did she know our secret?* They were the only ones talking. Everyone else stayed quiet to avoid saying something that might piss Diddy off. Even though the tense vibe was nothing new, I felt jumpy.

I fingered the gold cross that hung from my neck. Sister Mary Therese was the nicest nun I'd ever met. Every few Saturdays, she patiently taught me piano at Les Soeurs de Notre Dame de Bon Conseil Convent. She gave me sweet cinnamon fish-shaped candies and miniature bibles, no matter how crappy my playing was. But since yesterday, when Diddy confessed that we were actually Jewish, I wondered what she now thought.

Sean, who was two years younger than me, was spooning soup into his mouth, slurping like he was in a trance. I assumed that he had no idea about our hidden family history since Diddy said that my age was the reason he finally decided to tell me about it. I was dying to talk to him about it, but I took Dad's strict warning to heart. I was positive that at least some of my other siblings knew, because they were all older. Did they, like Diddy, live in fear of being killed? Was that the normal, grown-up way to feel? I chewed the nail on my forefinger, already bitten to the quick, silently praying that no one in our family had spilled the beans to an outsider and attracted what I was sure would be physical harm, if not death to us.

I raised my head to peek out through the opening in the curtains. Did it feel as tense inside other people's homes? Momma always said, "We don't need the neighbors looking in."

Highland Avenue was lined with nice brick houses, colored Christmas lights blinking from cozy-looking rooms and lawns decorated with Santa cut-outs and sleighs. Our living room contained the same holiday things every year. An artificial tree with only a few branches decked out with thin tinsel and barely any ornaments. Sometimes stockings were hung, but they were rarely filled. One year, mom put a few oranges in them, which we whined about, then returned to the crisper. It seemed like mentioning anything to do with Jesus' birthday depressed her. Now I understood why. She was sick of pretending to be Catholic.

Diddy coughed snapping my thoughts back to the dinner table, where a portion of pot roast lay on my plate. Momma must've come back into the dining room with the main course and to refill our glasses with milk, but I hadn't noticed. I cut through the ropey meat. I popped a portion into my mouth. As usual, the pot roast was a little tough, but after a lot of grinding, it was soft enough to be swallowed.

But Diddy, his mouth half-open, chomped the meat, then spat it into the cloth hanky he kept in his pocket. It grossed me out. Then he growled. "Liesel this food is so leathery, it could be sold to Swiss mountain climbers as beef jerky!"

I wondered how he could be so mean?

Comedy Club Palm Beach 2018

So anybody here have a mom and dad? Wow, well what are the chances! Lemme tell ya, it's hard when parents fight nonstop – my dad wanted to be Catholic, my mom wanted to be Jewish, I wanted to be adopted. Anyway, my Mom would rebel and it'd come out in her cocktails. So, my Dad would take a sip and go; (uptight enunciation) "Liesel, what did you put in the eggnog? It's absolutely revolting!" And she'd say; (Yiddish accent) "Uch Bernie, it's delicious. I spiked it...with Manischevitz!" – It's hard for immigrants because understandably it takes a while to adapt to a new culture and they had just

survived the war in Europe so to them food represented survival. So when my mom cooked a chicken she cooked every single part – NOTHING was thrown out. And we never had junk food, so the American custom of giving candy out at Halloween confused her. The neighborhood kids would be like "Dingdong! Trick or treat?" And my mom would go (German-Yiddish accent) "Oh vunderful Batman costume Little Henry! Open your bag - here's a REAL treat!" (Kid screams) "And a gizzard and a chicken foot for Little Sally!"(Little girl screams) "Sally, vy you run away?" And then my mom would run after them "Wait! Wait! I haven't given you za best part – za chicken head! You have no idea how delicious it is!" And they'd go "Frannie's mother's a REAL witch!" So our house became super popular at Hallowe'en which kept my parents from fighting for a few minutes. Y'know some people claim that when it comes to race they don't see color. You're white, black, brown whatever – in my case, having been raised Jewish and Catholic, I didn't see religion at home. But oh, did I hear religion! "Oh those Jews!" "Oy those Catholics!" My parents were always on opposing sides. But what relaxed me was when a Jehovah's Witness knocked because at least we were all on the same side of the door. I'm telling ya with the fighting that went on between them at home it's like the war never ended – really! And the weirdest thing about being raised Jewish and Catholic is BOTH religions think they're the ONLY good one! It's like being on the TV show *Survivor* – the Rabbi's like (Jewish accent) "Listen, us Jews survived the inquisition, plagues and the Holocaust – you think we can't handle being on an island at 110 degrees with hyenas? It's no different than being on Miami Beach with lawyers! The chosen people ARE gonna be the chosen winners!" And the priests are like (Irish accent) "Well Rabbi, we'll see how much heat your furry Jewish bottom can withstand when ya end up in the fiery pit of hell! 'Cuz, it's where you'll go for not followin' the one true God, Jesus, and that's why we Catholics are the winners!"

It's crazy-making growing up in the middle of a battlefield – my parents constantly fed us stories about people who starved to death during the war so dinner time with my six brothers and sisters was scary; forks were weapons - I'm surprised I have both eyeballs. It was like a feeding frenzy for komodo dragons!

Chapter 7

But that day at the dinner table, all I knew was heartburn. And I felt sorry for Momma who had spent hours cooking, and then served us like a slave. She just stared numbly as he laughed at his joke, straightening his dessert fork on the table, while the rest of us continued to chew. Then Momma slowly walked into the kitchen, as the door squeaked on its hinges.

We knew from having tried to defend Momma a few times before, that it would only irritate Diddy more. I dawdled at the table, torn between wanting to escape to my room and tempted by the smell of freshly baked pound cake coming from the kitchen. My salivating mouth called the shots, so I waited. And I watched my family, trying to figure out who might be the best person to approach for more information about our deadly secret. As usual, nobody was speaking. We never knew what might set Diddy off.

Angelic-looking, blue-eyed Sean sat next to me chewing hard on the rubbery meat. My little brother had a nervous habit, what Diddy called a compulsion. Between gulps of milk, he repeatedly patted and smoothed his perfectly folded damp linen napkin. Every now and then I tried to poke it, but he smacked away my finger "Fran-ces!" Clearly, Sean would be no help. I wanted to tell him what dad had told me, but knew that it would be unfaithful.

Marcus, two years older than me, sat opposite, lost in playing the air piano on the table, a melody which it seemed only he could hear. Since he was older than me, I was certain that Diddy had told him about our dangerous secret. Feeling me stare at him with intensity, made him look up. He blew me a kiss. It made me smile.

"You okay, Frannie?" he whispered.

I nodded, wondering whether his soft-heartedness made him feel extra icky about our family? I mulled over the best way to bring up the sneaky subject with him, maybe if I caught him alone in one of his bouncy moods.

"You sure?" he asked again.

I ignored him for a second, and instead glanced at Diddy. Seeing that Diddy was still occupied with Sally, I quickly hissed at Marcus "Do you know?"

"Huh?" shrugged Marcus.

I felt Diddy looking at me, and turned towards him. I gulped, uncertain if it he'd heard. But he had already looked away. Still, his gaze had freaked me out.

"What, Frances?" Marcus asked, annoyed.

"Uh – do you know what the uh – capitol of, no I mean the uh–" My cheeks felt hot. I found a breath, and pushed on, suddenly thinking of one of the books I was reading. "Do you know why the Grinch stole Christmas?"

"He stole it just to bug you!" Sean interrupted, sticking his tongue out at me. "Right, Marcus?"

Marcus laughed "Ex-actly Seany!"

I exhaled, relieved that they were teasing me. Then, I shifted my body away from them, pretending to be suddenly absorbed by looking at my sister Martha, hoping that they'd get distracted with each other. My blonde, green-eyed sis' was eleven years older than me. She had come home from university where she was a freshman, for a semester break. *Did she know? She must, since she's older.* She smiled at me. "Finished?" she asked pointing to my plate, before I could think how to question her. I nodded as she picked mine up, then stood and collected everyone's. She brought them to the kitchen. When she returned, she stood behind me. She opened my braids, which un-brushed looked like a photograph of squid ink fusilli I had seen in a coffee table book at my best friend Nancy's house. Martha combed my hair with her fingers making me sparkle. Still, I felt too shaky to try to question anyone in front of dad again. I decided that the next time she and I were alone I would ask her opinion about our family secret.

My eyes fell on Phillip, who was thirteen years older than me. He rarely stayed for dinner when Diddy was around to avoid his mood swings. I figured that he was lonely for us because most people got together with their relatives around Christmas. Momma had convinced him to stay. I was fond of my biggest brother, but since he had moved away from home before I'd been born, we didn't really know each other. He had recently adopted a French persona, grown a moustache, and started calling himself 'Philippe'. I liked how sophisticated he seemed. Still, the thought of having a private chat with him about our family felt weird. I just wasn't close enough to him to risk it. But I wondered whether he felt as lost as I did about who he really was? He squeezed in next to mother's empty chair, sitting directly across from dad, like a handsome stranger. Marcus had taken a break from playing the imaginary piano and they were eye-locked in a staring contest. It was an ongoing game they shared.

Diddy had stopped talking to Sally. Both the twins' faces were buried in medical books. Sally was studying to become a doctor. Madalen a pharmacist. From having annoyed them in the past by interrupting their reading, I now took the sharp points of their black cat-eye glasses to be automatic *Do Not Disturb* signs. Book-ending Diddy, they looked like super-intelligent bodyguards. They were twenty-four and completely identical. They had mother's narrow chin, her dark eyes, and both wore their hair in a stylish bob. Diddy often confused them, blending them into one mixed daughter, who he called "Sally-I-mean-Madalen-I-mean-Sally Oygevalt!" His slip-up always made me giggle.

I hoped that they would have some tips about how to get by in a world that was bad to Jewish people. I'll find a good time later today to ask them, I told myself. I lay my head on Madalen's shoulder, inhaling the sweet fumes wafting from the kitchen, as she softly patted my cheek.

"Safe, safe" I whispered to myself.

"Did you say something? Madalen asked.

"No – I must be *shpieling* – babbling. I'm starving!"

But the moment I said *shpieling*, I became self-conscious. *Maybe, it was actually a Jewish word? Or a European word like I had thought before?* I looked at Diddy and reminded myself to ask him later. He seemed lost in thought, looking gloomy.

For a moment, I remembered a photograph I had seen of him with mom when they were young holding my matching eldest sisters, one in each lap. Momma's dark eyes are shining and happy. I very rarely saw her looking anything close to that cheerful. Diddy eyes have a spark in them, like he just won a prize and can't believe it. They are both wearing suits and their shoulders touch. They seem relaxed.

Just then, mom came back into the dining-room. I jerked into sitting up. "Bernie, children, I apologize but Momma put the cake in too late," she said speaking about herself in the third person. "–and Momma forgot to make the icing. So, take a good twenty minutes, and when you return to the table, I promise you a nice dessert."

"That will be a miracle!" Diddy murmured, as we got up and headed to different places in the house. His comment made my tummy twist inside, but I straightened up and took a big breath, trying to pretend he hadn't said anything.

Chapter 8

Sally stood silently washing the dishes. I leaned on the counter and dried. Momma hummed while organizing the spice rack. She tested the top of the cooling pound cake with her finger, then sort of smiled and headed upstairs. Sally handed me a plate, a bowl, and a handful of forks. Dad who I'm pretty sure had been waiting in the hallway until mom left the kitchen, waltzed in and stood near the door. "Girls, meet me downstairs in my study. Quickly! I have very important things to discuss with you!"

"We're not done here," said Sally, but I was happy enough to leave the boring task of cleaning up, especially if it meant time alone with Diddy. I also felt not quite right in my skin. I wasn't sure who I was any more. I longed for Diddy to tell me some things to make me feel better.

The basement room was lined with shelves and filled with hundreds of books: Sigmund Freud's 'Interpretation Of Dreams';' The Rise And Fall Of The Third Reich' by William Shirer, and 'The Desk Reference For Ophthalmic Physicians' were the three that I remember. Once, while dad was at work, Sean and I had discovered How A Baby Is Made. We flipped through it but the pictures made us squirm.

The curtain covering the small window in our cellar was always streaked with dirt and closed. The basement smelled like mold and oak. Diddy's antique desk was dark and heavy and there was a stain on the brown carpet. Momma kept the rest of the house incredibly clean. But she never came down here. There was also a small bathroom, so Diddy didn't have to come up to the rest of the house except for meals.

I heard the toilet flush. Quickly, before the bathroom door could slide open, I hopped onto dad's chair, pretending to read 'Grants Atlas of Anatomy, 1970', which lay open on his desk. I'd been faking interest in Diddy's medical things 'cause I told him that I planned to follow in his footsteps and become an eye surgeon. I didn't dare let on that the smells and sights of the hospital made my stomach lurch, especially after I'd watched him perform an experimental operation on a rabbit's eye. I had willed myself to breathe through the whole thing by remembering all the goodies Diddy had given me because he was so excited about my wanting to go in to medicine; Almond bark and jellied half-moons from the candy store downtown, jumbo shrimp cocktails at a fancy restaurant, and presents, especially, a remote-control plush pink poodle I'd named Fifi-soso-lala.

I heard someone coming down the stairs. Sally walked into the library the same time as I heard Diddy glide the bathroom door open. "Is Frances with you?" Then he saw me, hunched over the big book. "Ah, jah. She's already here." He glanced over my shoulder, saw that I was reading about foot fungus, and said what he always said: "Good girl, study, study hard! You always want to be ahead of the game. They can take everything from you but they can never take away your knowledge!"

Sally sneezed. "Dusty!" she said, fishing for a tissue in the pocket of the sweater she'd decorated with embroidered flowers and blew her nose.

"Jah, your mother doesn't clean just to taunt me! Silly woman!" Sally and I moved our chairs so that they faced him. "You see, girls, sadly your own mother is not to be trusted! Her naiveté has led her to side with her brother, Gerd, the big Rabbi," Diddy exaggerated sarcastically "against me."

I wondered what a 'rabbi' was. I found it hard to believe that mom was consciously trying to annoy dad. I looked to Sally, who sat tight-lipped. I opened my mouth to speak, but she gave a very quick shake of the head, so I didn't say anything. I guessed that at one time she had tried to defend mom and was tipping me off that challenging Diddy was useless.

He kept talking, not really looking at us but more like he was delivering a speech. "Rabbi means teacher, Frances. Like a Jewish priest. You can see the difference with how they dress. Your uncle wears a yarmulke, uh – the small round hat." He cleared his throat. "Sadly, he sides with your mother and they join forces against me. Because I am such a bad man." He hissed, then kept talking like he was making fun of our family and Momma in a mean way. "That I try to protect my family! They blindly fight me tooth and nail, they think to be openly Jewish in this world is worth having your family murdered. She forgets what happened to her own mother – that her other brother Alfred had been sent to *Sachsenhausen*. She doesn't care that she sides with the enemy. But girls, you will always be able to trust me – but only me."

"Diddy, what happened to Momma's mother?" I asked. I hadn't expected my voice to tremble.

Sally pointed to a black-covered book on the shelf behind her. "See this book? Page 582. It's seared into my brain."

Ah-hah. She knows way more than I do about our family, I thought.

Just then, she saw dad's brow furrow. Her mouth opened slightly, then she quickly said, "Uh, Diddy, should you perhaps tell Frances about our family history in *'The Rise And Fall Of The Third Reich'*?"

Diddy took a big breath, and exhaled, "Jah – another time, my sweethearts. That is enough for now. And we don't want to miss your mother's attempt at dessert! Hard to mangle the taste of a freshly baked cake, but somehow she always manages to do just that!"

Diddy's split-second shift from talking about murder to sweets made me dizzy. And my gut cringed. I didn't want to hear him complain about Momma anymore.

I peeked at Sally. She was listening, her hands folded on her lap. Seeing me look at her, Diddy said, "Your sister Sally is the only one besides me who you can go to, Frances. Who you can trust. Your mother has brainwashed all the other children and they will turn against you in a heartbeat. It's a very sad thing to hear, that your own mother, your brothers and sisters, are dangerous, but better you find out sooner than later."

I skimmed through my siblings in my mind. I loved all of them. Hearing that they were untrustworthy bummed me out. Yet knowing that Diddy trusted me gave me some strength. I wasn't sure what had made him decide that he could feel safe with me and Sally, or why exactly mom wanted to stay Jewish even though it was dangerous, but I was too nervous to try to find out.

"You understand Frances?" I nodded but my heart wasn't totally in it. I was sure that this was not the first time dad had warned Sally about our enemies. "We will go spend some nice time together on the weekend, my girls. Get some French pastries, or go to the Viennese cafe and Frances, we will go to the toy store on Thursday. Jah, let's make it a habit on Thursdays. Just keep all the things I share with you to yourself! Don't worry! Diddy will make up for the bad feelings at home. And most importantly–" Diddy pointed at me. He wagged his finger from side to side, "Frances you especially need to take this to heart; Sally knows only too well the harm that can befall her from opening her mouth. Never, ever, tell anyone, that you are Jewish!"

I wasn't sure if she agreed with Diddy or if she always swallowed her opinion around him, but I now knew better than to ask her in front of him.

I was dazed by dad's belief that our home was such a horrible place. Sure, sometimes Momma was unkind and cried but I figured it was because Diddy could be so nasty. I couldn't imagine that mother, who was so super protective, would cause us harm on purpose. But Diddy had been so intense when he was warning us, that I was pretty sure there was some truth to it. My world at home felt like it was split in two.

And as for Uncle Gerd, I had met him once and he seemed very sweet. Plus, he made a great fashion statement! He always wore what I had then thought was a beanie, but now I knew it was a yarmulke. But my head hurt knowing that he was willing to risk our family getting killed. I felt so yucky I could hardly sit still. So, I escaped the best way I knew how.

I searched the room for something to stare at. My eyes fell on a can of reel-to-reel films Diddy had stashed in the cupboard. I scrunched my eyes and tried to remember scenes from one of the Charlie Chaplin films we'd watched. Dad's favorite was 'The Great Dictator.' When Charlie Chaplin played a short man with a bristly mustache, dad had screamed with laughter.

"Diddy, do you think maybe we can see a movie sometime again? Like the one we went to a long time ago, 'Funny Girl,' remember?"

I had been dazzled by Barbara Streisand playing a jolly, glamorous woman. It was as if when she was up there on the screen, she was everything that my childhood home wasn't. At that moment, I decided to become an actress. I hadn't told anyone about my feelings but now, something in me was pulled to.

"Diddy, do you think I could be an actress too?"

Diddy walked over to me, stroked my hair, and smiled down at me "That is such a sweet dream! Like the international actress, Anne Sheridan. Something to shoot for!"

My heart exploded. I looked at Sally. She smiled encouragingly.

"Yay. Diddy! I would love to grow up and be an actress!" I exhaled. I almost said 'Phew' out loud. I was so relieved that Diddy hadn't gotten pissed off that I didn't want to become an eye surgeon anymore.

Chapter 9

Less than twenty minutes later, we had all returned to our places at the dining room table. My tummy still had butterflies from Diddy's nice reaction.

Momma carried in a covered porcelain dessert platter announcing, "Lemon macaroon flavor this time. Frances, your favorite!"

But before I could answer Diddy roared. "Frances, don't eat that poison!" Then Mom took the lid off the plate of yellow frosted pound cake. Diddy squinted at it. "What is this now, Liesel? It looks like urine on snow." He turned to face everyone at the table. "Last time I ate your mother's baking, I had a bellyache you wouldn't believe!"

I chewed the skin around my thumb. A few minutes earlier, downstairs, dad had seemed almost happy.

Momma smiled but her upper lip was trembling. She spoke slowly and carefully. "Bernie, why so fresh? Children take a bite, it's delicious and lemon-y." I gritted my teeth. I was pleased that she had stuck up for herself. But would it make Diddy behave even worse?

Sean scarfed some cake before Momma had a chance to spit out, "Take, take!"

I snatched a piece but Diddy leaned over and slapped it out of my hand. "Listen to me!" He scolded as my dessert landed on the table and fell apart. "Your mother wants to go against my wishes and side with the enemy. You have no idea what toxin she tries to put in us. Frances, Sally I take you to the Viennese Café afterwards."

I expected Momma to say something but she didn't. She was squishing her lips together. I felt like I had to pee. This was the first time I heard Diddy accuse Momma of being the enemy, to her face. I began to whimper. Diddy ignored me so I increased to big, loud, snotty sobs I wanted everyone to hear. It felt like no one in the room was breathing and it was comforting to know that they were all listening to me. Still, I wanted to go to mom and hold her. But I could hardly look at her.

She smoothed her apron. Finally, she took a seat at the table. "Bernie, you're way over the line! We need to see someone – a psychiatrist. Together. We nee–"

"I can teach any psychiatrist a thing or two!" Diddy barked. "Sigmund Freud was my teacher! And Freud's daughter, Anna, as you well know, Liesel, is my good friend. How dare you!"

Comedy Club Palm Beach 2018

Are you two guys in the front married? Dating? No? Really! Secretly lusting? I knew it! It's weird, but if you trust your gut you can always tell when people are lying. Like when two people who you're pretty sure are romantically involved, say; "We're just good friends" it's always suspect –like my Dad would have this odd smile whenever he'd say that he and Freud's daughter Anna were "just good friends", but I dunno; I found a photograph of them and from the possessive way she's looking at him she wasn't suffering from any penis-envy. Nunh-unh she owned his *shmekel* – penis! My dad actually studied with the famous Siggy at the University of Vienna, so I was inundated with Freudian theories practically from birth, which actually benefitted me greatly. In kindergarten during naptime I'd diagnose my classmates and they'd pay me with M&M's. I'd be like (Yiddish intonation) "Sally, za reason you don't have a favorite Barbie doll reflects a deep neurotic disparity between your super ego and your id." She'd go "Okay whatever! How many red ones do I owe you today?" Listen, kids imitate their parents – and my dad revered all things that had to do with Freud. So, I did too - during Halloween I went door to door in bad neighborhoods giving psychiatric advice in exchange for cocaine.

Then I'd attend Narcotics Anonymous meetings for the free cookies. Of course I developed a cookie addiction, which actually benefitted me as an adult because if someone pisses me off instead of saying "You @#% idiot!" I just say "Wanna cookie?!"

Chapter 10

So when I was nine years old, since I knew that Freud was a bigshot who Diddy had known, I could understand why Diddy felt like he had a handle on things. Even though I secretly knew he didn't. I decided to ask Diddy more about Freud later to make him feel better.

Momma sighed, smoothing the tablecloth. "Your dad is in a bad mood again. Please don't let the lovely lemon-macaroon cake go to waste." She leaned over and swept the crumbs off the table into her cupped hand, then nibbled them. "Mm-mm, delicious!" She took a slice and placed it on Phillip's plate. "Enjoy! Children, pass me your dishes."

Sally and I didn't budge, feeling too closely watched by our prickly dad.

Momma reached for our plates. "Bernie, we need to give the children a nice feeling of cozy family, what we used to have–" She switched to German and continued talking in their private language.

Diddy snarled in English. "Community? You want community? Fine. I'll give them community!" He spread his hands wide, suddenly smiling. "Children, how would you three little ones like to spend time at camp this summer? Go canoeing, swimming, make arts and crafts?"

I hadn't realized I'd been holding my breath until I exhaled. I had expected Diddy to shout at mom again. We had never heard him talk about attending summer camp. I noticed that Momma was looking at him strangely. She had cocked one of her jet-black eyebrows.

"Right on, swimming!" hooted Marcus.

"Sounds like fun for you guys!" said Madalen.

"Canoeing...wooh!" said Sally, wide-eyed.

"Okay, I tell you what, Liesel," Diddy said as if he was giving Momma the best gift in the world. "I heard from some other doctors about the good times their children had at Camp Katimavik. I will register our three youngest for the summer program."

Momma took a balled-up tissue from her sleeve and began carefully wiping the edges of the table. After a moment, she softly spoke. "Lovely, but Bernie it's months early for summer camp – you know what I meant. I want us to celebrate who we are!"

I wasn't sure exactly what she wanted us to celebrate, but I knew that it had to do with being Jewish. I took a small breath. I didn't want Diddy to notice. I was dying to know about the missing part of me.

Diddy roared something in German at Momma. She made throaty noises while shaking her head 'no' and dabbing the edges of the cake platter with her tissue. He continued, wagging his forefinger. Although I could only understand bits and pieces like "Juden" which I knew meant Jews, and "Monstrum" which meant monsters, I knew that dad was talking about creepy things that happened to Jews. I looked down in case Diddy was going to make eye contact. The hair on my arm was standing straight up. Still, I was aching to know more about the secret.

Diddy finished his lecture. "I will not be taken for a fool, Liesel! And don't you dare bring danger here with your naive, blind trust. You know very well what happened to those who believed that things would get better–"

Momma started speaking in the same calming tone she spoke to me in when I had a temper tantrum. "Bernie, things have been fine here for many years. We just need to connect and join some social groups maybe join a nice synagogue."

"Things are getting bad again all over, Liesel. I've been watching the news. Jew-haters are springing up like daisies." Diddy threw his napkin down, and got up quickly. He crossed the dining room and went downstairs. Nobody spoke. Momma nibbled on a piece of cake. The moment we heard the sound of dad's study door closing, all us kids stood. I glanced at Momma, who was nodding to herself. I could tell she was trying to stay calm.

"Move out, troops!" commanded Marcus playfully, freeing us to scatter to our separate, safe places in the house.

I didn't understand everything Diddy had said to mother over dinner, but from then on, whenever I heard him, or anyone else say the word 'Jew', it shone at me as harshly as what I imagined was a Nazi search light.

Chapter 11

Thirty years later, undulating my hips under the fluorescent stage lights, onstage at the strip bar, I squirmed as the audiences excited outbursts subsided. I felt suddenly over-exposed. The side of my cheek smarted reminding me that I'd been gnawing it. I smiled broadly, covering my annoyance, still miffed that earlier, I had gotten such a lousy response when I'd revealed my udder G-string. But I was able to console myself that in general I was being admired for baring parts of myself, and I basked in that good feeling of spicy freedom.

Holding onto the pole with my thighs and hands, I swung myself around with tremendous momentum, then arched my back while sliding my legs higher until I was almost upside down. Now grabbing the pole tightly with my legs, I spun as I descended to the ground, unhooking my bra with one hand as I went. As it dangled from my shoulders, the men pounded their fists on the stage, saluting the appearance of my breasts, as my golden nipple tassels danced. The thousands of jazz classes I'd taken over the years were finally coming in handy. I decided to attempt another new trick. Back rolling to where I'd positioned the glass of ice, I selected a cube. 'Crucify' by Tori Amos began to play. This time I didn't hear any comments, because the culturally challenged component of the crowd had stopped paying attention to the music. I unfurled myself like the skin of an apple being run through a peeler, and danced into an upright position while I pressed the melting cube up and down on my warm cleavage. My audience catcalled in a deafening sound when my moistened flesh steamed under the lights, making me giggle unexpectedly. It was startling to hear myself laugh so playfully at the same time as I was acting sexual in public. Yet, somehow it caused me to feel instantly calmer and protected. I felt fiercely free.

I removed my open bra and tossed it over my shoulder towards the back of the stage. I shook it over to the pole and squeezed my uneven breasts together around it to occupy their attention, grateful for this illusion device. All the oxygen in the room had been replaced by cigarette smoke and the men stared bug-eyed as if in a trance. It made me think of a time when my dad had trapped me into listening to yet another one of his dark stories.

Chapter 12

That night, Diddy had woken me suddenly. By now, he had interrupted my sleep so many times that my body always jolted awake when hearing the slightest noise. I got up and peeked out the door. He was carrying sheets and pillows into the spare bedroom. I shut my door quietly, wondering how mother was.

About twenty minutes later, dad opened my door. "Frances, come into my room!" he whispered. I had been sleeping heavily, and would have preferred to catch more shut-eye, but I got up and followed him, rather than risk him getting snarly.

I saw that he had made up one of the two empty beds, which my sisters had slept on when they still lived at home. "Now you sit down Frances, and you listen to me." I could tell by his tone that he was more freaked out than usual. He peeked out into the hallway, then closed the door. I perched on the unmade bed. "I've been watching the news and reading the papers and I am certain that another Holocaust is brewing just around the corner."

My head felt hot. I didn't want to believe it. "Like with the Nazis and everything?" I searched for a way to lighten things up while dad nodded, sucking in his lower lip. He came over, bent down, and held both my hands in his.

"And Frances, I want you to know that if we are so poor one day that we are living in a one room shack, I put a division down the room, and you are on one side and I on the other and if we are so poor with only one potato to eat, I take that potato and I cut it in half and–"

"Diddy, growing carrots like I do in the summer every year could help too, right?"

He took a breath and smiled realizing I was serious. "Sweet girl, very nice."

"Actually, the carrots Momma made for the stew last night were the ones I picked from my garden last week!"

"Very nice, Sweetheart."

Chapter 13

"Nice shot, Sweetheart!" a gravelly male voice shouted, from the side of the strip club stage.

I turned in his direction. An old man wearing filthy coveralls stood by himself twirling my bra lasso-style. Shit! My aim was always crappy.

Slithering in his direction, I quipped in my faux British; "Hey handsome, be a love and toss that up to me?"

He wasn't having any of it. As I drew closer a feces-like aroma overwhelmed me. The reason for his isolation became clear. He must have been a farmer who had come to the club directly from slopping out the pig sty without passing go or a wash basin. Drooling into his beer, he grinned at me through teeth that appeared to consist of pieces of old banana peels. He placed my bra on the stage close to him, rubbing his crotch with his other hand, shouting, "Come to Daddy, come to Daddy!"

Chapter 14

Back in what was now his bedroom, dad bulldozed ahead. "Okay, listen to Diddy now. I have seen things you should never have to. I was saying that if we are so impoverished, God forbid, that we have only one potato, you will have enough to eat. I will share it with you. And Frances, if I am an old man and I am unable to wash my personal parts, I want you to know that it is the good and decent thing for a daughter to do for her old dad that–"

I was choking, couldn't catch a breath. "Diddy, Diddy–" I gulped air. "Do we have to talk about this? Isn't there something else we can talk about?"

Without taking a second to consider, he slowly replied, arms wide, eyes watery. "Who else do I have to talk to?"

I wanted to reject Diddy, but it felt way too selfish, even though the mere thought of his privates made my stomach cave. For a second I considered giving him an excuse about my having to use the bathroom, but I could barely breathe. I continued to behave like a good girl, sitting still on the side of the bed next to his, even though I was queasy. He took a moment to pace and think. I took a breath. He turned towards me and opened his mouth to say something. Just then, we heard what sounded like music coming from somewhere in the house. At first, I wasn't sure if I was imagining it. But when dad opened the door, piano notes drifted upstairs from the living room.

I peeked out into the hallway and saw Sean. "What is Marcus doing now?" he whined.

Dad headed downstairs, past mother who was standing in her nightgown, in her doorway. "Bernie, he may be sleepwalking!" she warned.

I crept after dad, watching through the rails of the bannister, praying that he wouldn't lose it.

Marcus was lit by a lamp, sitting at the piano. He glimpsed Diddy entering the living room, but didn't stop playing. Dad turned on the main light, causing Marcus to play faster. "Get away from me!" said Marcus.

I was relieved to see Diddy stay calm. "Mark-y, calm yourself! Son, you play beautifully, but what gives you the right to wake up the entire household? I have surgery very early and everyone has school and so on."

Marcus started to pound the keys faster and faster. "Don't make me stop or they will get me! You are looking at me with lop-sided lips!"

I realized that Marcus was behaving extremely oddly, but couldn't tell if it was an act or not. Dad approached the piano. "What nonsense you talk! You are acting like a crazy person!" Now he sounded impatient.

Marcus shouted, his eyes frantic. "You've distracted me! That's it, they're going to punish me for being bad, for having dirty thoughts! Thanks a lot!" He got up, banged the piano lid shut, and stomped up the stairs, grunting as he passed me, then slammed the door to his bedroom behind him. Sean went in and closed the door to our bedroom.

Something secret in me enjoyed Marcus's anger. Dad turned off the lights and began climbing the stairs. Edgy, I stood and said, "Diddy, don't get upset, but I think Marcus really does think he's crazy, because–"

"Because?" demanded dad.

"Because you keep telling him so, Bernie!" Momma said, finishing my sentence for me. I had almost forgotten that she was standing there.

"Ach, nonsense! You hear this terrible accusation, Frances? She tries to turn the children against me!" Diddy shouted after Momma as she shut the door to their bedroom. "The boy is crazy, like his mother!" He walked towards what was his new bedroom, at least for tonight. "I'm wide-awake now." He waved for me to follow him.

I almost sighed out loud as I entered after him, closed the door and balanced on the edge of a chair. He stood, staring at the door, shaking his head. Then he paced, repeatedly finger-combing oily wisps of hair, nervously pulling on his beard with the other hand. "The boy has problems – it's his mother's doing, Frannie, her crazy ways, confusing him, questioning me all the time. He doesn't know what's up or what's down anymore. But I am a good man –"

Diddy stood still and pointed in the direction of Momma's room. "Not like some people whose names I won't mention! No matter what they tell you Frances, I do everything to protect you and our whole family. I always did. I tried so hard to save my parents, I–"

Dad's voice grew thin as he pulled back a sob. "When I meet my maker, he will know that I am innocent! And the worst thing is, your mother has turned Madalen against Sally – a terrible thing to do to a twin."

He turned towards me. "Be careful with what you share with anyone other than Sally, or me, Frances! When you are not looking they report everything to their mother who tells them what a bad man I am. How terrible I am that I try to guard the family from certain danger! But don't worry Frances, we have each other, always."

I yawned forcefully hoping that it would make dad want to get to the end of his story. He scrunched his brows at me. "Sorry, Diddy."

"Now you listen to me, they would like to prove me a traitor, a Jew. But they will never get me because they have no proof. Nothing. Frannie, I will keep you away from your mother's grip, we will take care of each other."

Both Diddy and I jumped at a noise we heard outside the door. He placed a finger to his lips. He tiptoed to the door, then swooped it open. Momma stood outside, her ear turned sideways, eavesdropping. "What are you doing here, you crazy woman?" he shouted. He looked at me, stabbing the air. "You see? She spies on us! What do you expect to find here crazy woman? How dare you!"

My stomach knotted. I wanted to go to Momma and hug her. But was she bad? What if Diddy was right? Maybe he was the only one I could rely on. Once again it felt as if my heart was being sawed in half.

Mom craned her neck, peering into the room past dad, at me. "Is Frances okay? I'm just worried that she'll be too tired for school in the morning."

"Don't make up stories, Liesel. You know who you are!" Diddy said, smirking.

Momma locked eyes with him. "I tell the truth about who I am, Bernie!"

Diddy moved into the hallway, causing mother to back up. "Get out of here or I'll have you put away!"

"I go, I go." Momma escaped to her room. I was grossed-out being stuck in that room with Diddy.

"One day you'll be sorry!" dad yelled in her direction, re-entering the room, red-faced. "You see that Frances? Your mother spies, causes trouble – she is crazy! You can only trust me. But I will always be here for you, Frances." He exhaled, slumping his shoulders. "Diddy needs to sleep now." He pecked me on the cheek, then yawned nonstop.

"Good night, Diddy" I said, relieved to be going back to my room. Although I was too tired to think, I sensed something was very wrong. I couldn't put my finger on it, but I felt like I was smeared in something disgusting, like the time I dropped my necklace in the toilet and when I fished it out it was full of poop.

But as a young girl, though my father's behavior revolted me, deep down I blamed myself for not being able to deal with it better. Of course, I didn't know how unabashedly inappropriate he was being. Having been groomed to be his good daughter, I weighed far more heavily towards feeling responsible for his emotional well-being than my own. Ions later one of the things which helped me feel less like damaged goods was when I realized that I wasn't alone in my experience.

_____

https://www.quora.com/Do-you-feel-you-have-been-emotionally-raped-by-someone

Chapter 15

I never felt as dirty while working as a stripper as I did in dads room. And I felt pretty slutty. But, the primary discomfort which reverberated, was that someone in the crowd might recognize me from the press I'd received for my play about my family. Then, I'd be outed as a Jew. And then, depending on how anti-Semitic this crowd was, who knows what horror might befall me? But with each item of clothing I removed my trepidation diminished.

I had compiled an eclectic selection of songs to strip to, the likes of what the stunned Gentleman's club crowd seemed never to have heard during a dancer's act. Ricky Martins "La Vida Loca" blared. I burst into a super-fast salsa. Nobody and nothing was going to stop me from expressing myself now. The song ended. I stood, heart racing, staring down the audience. They looked confused by my Hispanic aerobics. The other strippers only moved slowly and seductively onstage while I delighted in the occasional endorphin buzz. But as Sinead O'Connor began singing "I am stretched on your grave" I took the opportunity which the slow song allowed; to make my enslaved audience wait even longer for me to finish my untraditional antics, while incrementally undressing.

"The shit that's playing now's even worse!" some guy groaned.

I gyrated twice in the direction of an armless man in the front row, causing my gold shimmery nipple tassel pasties to sway.

"No way that those'r her real tits!" he hissed to no one in partic- ular. "Oh wait, they're whadda-ya-call them…pasties!"

"Bingo, cupcake!" I coo'd.

My right hip smarted, reminding me that I was standing off balance. I'd inherited scoliosis, which my dad had informed me had a carrier rate of 1 in 27 Ashkenazi Jews. It manifests in occasional radiated pain, exacerbated by physical activity. Holding onto the pole, I allowed my knees to bend so that the weight of my body stretched my hips. Zigzagging my way back up in an attempt to disguise my exercise as a seductive move, I came to stand with my back to the audience. I ran my hands over my ass several times as much to buy time as to be suggestive. Slowly, I turned to face my mesmerized posse, leaning the entire weight of my back on the pole. I crossed my arms massaging my breasts, flicked the tassels, then slowly pulled the pasties off.

"Oof bet that hurt!" quipped my critic.

"It hurt bloody good, Jellybean!" I shot back, tossing my pasties over my shoulder towards the back of the stage. Applying adhesive in a single spot above my nipples so that the removal was more tugging than painful, was a lesson I'd learned the hard way.

"Work it baby!" Boobra suddenly cheered from the side of the stage.

I hadn't noticed her there. From what she had divulged about her feminist academic studies, we were on the same socio-political side, and both driven to be truth-tellers. After meeting her earlier, I was tempted to try to impress her later with the success I'd had with my solo play in which I disclosed my deepest family secret. But I wasn't willing to risk the chance that she might turn on me. I had learned that some people came very well disguised. Besides Boobra and I hadn't even shared our real names. Although her alias was based on a Jewish celebrity, what if making fun of a Jew had been her goal and she was actually an anti-Semite? Although I didn't have a shred of evidence to support my fear, I'd heard many stories about the so-called friends of my parents who'd sold our relatives to the Nazis. There was a myriad of ways people could hurt you. What if she reported me as a Jew to the agents who'd booked me as a stripper? Again, I hadn't any reason to assume that they were racist. But I didn't think they needed much reason to fire me. At thirty-nine, although I still maintained the physique of a jazz dancer, I wasn't one of the most valued of their line-up stripping alongside primarily twenty and early thirty-somethings.

She beckoned me. I sashayed over to her as the horny men shouted, "Duo! Duo!"

FRANNIE SHERIDAN

"Want to?" she whispered, nodding. I could tell it hadn't been her first time.

"Um. Okey-doke Pet – but how?" I stuttered.

"Don't worry I'll just tease them on one side of the stage, and you go over there, and then we'll dance together for a minute and make a ridic amount of tips. Okay?"

"Right-o!" I said, nervously. "I was never asked to do this in the U.K." I quipped attempting to cover. Be playful, I reminded myself. As anxious as I was, I enjoyed the camaraderie from someone who was also publicly sharing something generally considered taboo.

"Hey handsome!" she shouted to the bartender "Smiley! We're doing a duo! Put on 'Hot Boys'."

The crowd went nuts. Boobra grabbed my hand and pulled me behind her as she paraded along the periphery of the stage. She was wearing thigh-high dominatrix boots. We shimmied together as the hollering of our onlookers rocketed. She let my hand go. I continued to boogie while she utilized the moment to step off the stage onto a table adjacent where an Armani-suited young man sat alone. Whistles crescendo'd. She lingered staring him down, barely wagging her hips as he gaped at her crotch, just inches from his head. Milking the moment, she slowly sank down, finally crouching in front of him, face to face. He fished for a bill, then whispered something to her while sticking two hundred-dollar bills in her cleavage.

Boobra ruffled his hair and stood. She turned to me shrugging, then hollered offstage, "Smiley! Does this sound like Missy Elliot to you?" She was right. The Sinead O'Connor song from my set was still playing.

"You know the rules! Duos need to be scheduled or you don't get paid for them," Smiley roared.

Boobra strutted towards the stairs. As she passed me she shook her head and hissed, "Patriarchal Bullshit!" making me snort a half-laugh.

I was amazed at her boldness. Before committing to work in a Gentleman's club, I had made a vow to myself to never vacate the clearly defined boundaries of the stage to entice. Other than my accent, I had decided that the rest of my professional sexy persona would dissolve the moment I stepped off the platform. I had been assured that the clientele was strictly forbidden to touch us

51

during our onstage performances, and the bouncers seemed highly dependable having assured me with, "Baby, other than the dancers, no asshole has ever set more than one foot on that stage before he gets his face ripped off!" Still, having crystal clear presentation boundaries helped me to feel not only physically but emotionally protected. And, I was relieved that those in the crowd who desired a more hands-on experience had options. A clearly identifiable tier of strippers wearing filmy see-through coverups over bare breasts, or sporting peek-a-boo bras, offered lap dances continuously strutting around the room, soliciting with, "Private dance, baby?" or winking at the introverts cooing things like, "…room in the back if you're shy." The more inebriated lap dancers simply plunked themselves onto the men's laps without invitation, then butt-humped their crotches, grinding with the hope that their captive male would become so turned on that they'd practically beg to pay so as to be able to climax inside their pants.

Although I respected the lap dancer's choices, the idea of having sexual interactions with customers other than providing a fantasy, sickened me. But I couldn't stop thinking about how luxurious it would be to make that amount of money so quickly. What if I was able to replicate the same feeling of safety that I already felt onstage to some degree, while I interacted offstage? Maybe then I could pull it off; if I approached dancing offstage as if it was an acting exercise. I could use my senses to remember what it felt like to be protected. Then, I could interact with the clientele in the same way that Boobra had. It felt enormously hazardous. I had learned from my experiences with dad that bad boundaries were corrosive.

Chapter 16

Diddy repeatedly said that mom was mentally ill and went on and on about what the Nazis had done to crazy people. I couldn't stop hearing his voice when he had told me that, "In mental institutions they use electrodes to give shock treatment to patients who are trapped inside. Sometimes they strap them down onto beds."

"But Diddy, why are they so horrible to people?" I asked.

"Some people are animals, Frances," he answered, nodding to himself, "But on the other hand, some psychiatrists are very well-intended, like my good friend Anna, and of course her esteemed dad."

I knew the 'dad' he was talking about was the famous psychiatrist who had been his teacher in Vienna. Sigmund. But even though Diddy said that some of the psychiatrists were decent like his friend was, it didn't make me feel any better. There were monsters out there. And I figured that being Momma's daughter, the chances were good that she had passed her craziness on to me. Some nights, I woke up from the same scary dream about being tortured in a dark building, my heart jumping out of my chest. So, studying mental illness became a serious hobby. I figured that somehow, what I learned would keep my nuttiness under control and maybe then if I had to, I could prove that I was sane. Still, I worried that I was a seriously bad kook and I couldn't stop the thought. It would eat at me, and shoot my tummy. I would stare at the cracking paint on the walls of our house. I wondered if in the same way that my stomach couldn't handle mental illness stories, that the horrid feelings inside our home became too much for the paint on the walls to handle? When I was feeling that out of control, I was sure that it was just a matter of time before I would be found out. A crazy Jewish-Catholic girl who's torn in half.

One day at St. Basil's school, I stood in front of our class holding up a large piece of bristle board. I had drawn pictures of heads with holes in them. We had been asked to create a project to do with health. After flipping through one of Diddy's historical medical atlases, I came across a topic which deeply shocked and inspired me. It seemed even worse than the horror I imagined might happen to Momma, should Diddy have her committed, so in a weird way it actually stopped me from worrying about her for a bit because I knew that this couldn't ever happen to her.

"Please explain your project," Mr. Lalonde said. I could tell by the way he was squinting at my bristle board and pressing his lips together, that he was concerned. But, I was sure that once he understood how interesting it was he would be impressed.

"This is called 'Trepanning'." Then I read the definition. "A surgical intervention popular in the 14th and 15th century, during which a hole is drilled or scraped into the human skull, exposing the dura mater to treat health problems related to intracranial diseases."

I smiled up at Mr. Lalonde. He was still staring at my artwork, but now his mouth was hanging open. I gazed around the class. Everyone was ogling the display in stunned silence. My head retracted into my neck like a turtle's. After a few moments which felt like hours, without looking at me, he quietly said, "Miss Sheridan, please resume your seat."

I did. Nobody said anything. I looked at my best friend Nancy, but she wouldn't make eye contact. They can't stand me. They think I'm insane. Stomach spirals. Oh no, they're going to lock me up. Just like Momma.

My assignment was inspired by one of my parents' recent arguments. Mom had been wiping the counters in the kitchen as dad paced outside the open kitchen door, tugging at a little beard he'd grown that looked a lot like the one in his photograph of his teacher, Doctor Freud.

"There are many anti-Semites, remember Frances, those are Jews-haters. Your mother knows this yet she tells her brother the bi-i-ig Rabbi, about how bad I am! For protecting us! Her behavior is very dangerous! She is going to get us in trouble, yet she doesn't care!"

Momma left the kitchen and began polishing the knotty pine wood paneled wall in our living room, close to the sofa where I was sitting. I pretended to leaf through the newspaper. Diddy, who had taken a few steps to keep a close distance, kept scolding her. I saw how trapped into listening to him she was. "How dare you go against me, you crazy woman!" he said, screwing up his face into a tight nub, so that his mouth became a small "o".

I couldn't help thinking that it looked exactly like the asshole on the pet cat I'd had a few years earlier. The comparison made me smile inside. But it was only momentary relief from the pervasive feelings of anxiety which were dominant at home.

Chapter 17

But back in my childhood home, my father continued to wield his 'asshole-holic' behavior.

"I will have you institutionalized! All it takes is one doctor's signature!"

Every iota of my body tightened hearing once again, that mom might have to live somewhere else. I wanted to defend her, but I knew it would make things worse. I started to hyperventilate. Diddy hurried over, telling me to breathe slowly. I took my time relaxing, wanting to give Momma some breathing space as well.

She took some magazines and headed upstairs. He followed her into the hallway, and then hollered after her. "Women who become hysterical like your crazy mother are sometimes given a brain operation called a frontal lobotomy to calm them, but afterwards they often had to live in an institution, like a big hospital. For life."

I wanted to scream, "Don't you dare, Diddy!" but I couldn't. I couldn't even make a sound. I thought about the muzzle that my best friend Nancy's German shepherd wore so that she wouldn't bite. And what I realized then, was that I didn't need leather to clamp my mouth shut. I was muzzled by terror. Every bit of me ached at the thought of Momma having someone open her head. "I know these things are hard to hear, Frances, but they are for your own protection. You need to know what's going on but you must keep them to yourself! I know many things about many people, but unlike your mother, I don't have a big mouth. Jewish, Jewish, she pushes to stay Jewish. At what cost? I will not lose another family!" He headed towards the basement stairs. "Come downstairs, Frances."

The walls felt too close to me – I was dying to run outside. But, I followed him. I knew he was going to give me yet another lecture, this time during the day.

Diddy closed the door to the study. I fiddled with the small handle on one of the drawers of his antique desk, wishing I could crawl inside, close the drawer, and lock myself in.

"If you talk against certain people Frances, you're done for! Sit." He pulled a chair close to me and continued whispering hoarsely. "There is a doctor in Montreal at a hospital, a psychiatric hospital – a place for people with problems, an institution. He's completely *meshuga* – crazy. Cameron. Very dangerous man! Now what I am telling you is top secret. Until now, I have never told you his name. You hear me Frances? People who are paid to do this work would kill you for less! Keep this to yourself, Frances!" He waited for my nod, then kept on yammering at me. "Cameron is supported by the CIA in forcing patients to take LSD. Many doctors know and just turn a blind eye – they won't even discuss it. The patients are given drugs that take you on a trip outside of your conscious state, Frances – like a terrible nightmare for them, in most cases – they call it a 'clinical trial', my *tuchas* – butt! Putting vulnerable and disturbed human beings in a comatose state for weeks and administering electroshock therapy. Fastening them to a bed, Frances, so they cannot escape and putting electrical currents through their bodies. They are brain damaged for life, often losing bowel functions and other things–"

My body felt as heavy as lead. Thoughts raced around my head. Once I'd gotten shocked plugging in the toaster. It scared the crap outta me. Tied to a bed and forced to feel that? For weeks? While having bad dreams?

Diddy pointed his forefinger at me. "You see Frances, I know all of this and as much as I would like to expose this barbarian, I would never talk and put my family at risk! One day it will all come out in the open. Believe me Frances, the less information people have about you the better! Do not be a big-mouthed Jew! The Nazis --" he paused searching for the right words. I was glad he'd taken a second break. By then I felt so soaked with hair-raising emotion. I couldn't absorb another poisonous-feeling drop.

What I remembered later from what he had said during the rest of his talk, was that Nazis had done terrible things to patients or even sometimes to people who were completely normal. "Experiments on many Jewsish twins," he said as he looked off into the distance. I could tell he was remembering. He looked like he was watching a movie playing in his head. "Dr. Mengele – jah. Another so-called doctor, an evil monster, beyond evil, sewing twins together with their own skin and bones at Auschwitz – like a terrible prison, you shouldn't have to know, Frances."

But it was too late. His stories made me shaky inside. I didn't want to be there when he told me. I didn't want to be anywhere. And from then on, whenever I saw a uniformed man, or a doctor, I imagined all the evil things he could do. I had recurring thoughts that wouldn't stop about awful things being done to Sally and Madalen. When I took my clothes off, I automatically thought about someone shocking my personal parts with electricity. Before I spoke to friends, or in class, I was afraid that someone would shoot me for saying the wrong thing. So, I spoke a lot less. I lay awake during the nights worrying. Maybe I had a hole in my head too?

Even worse than knowing that the world was full of evil people, waiting to tear me apart, was that I couldn't understand how dad, who I adored, who I wanted to always protect, could threaten to harm Momma. I got how much they disagreed about the Jewish stuff. But since Diddy had told me how horrific the doctor in Montreal who did brain tests on mentally challenged people was, I was beyond blown away that he threatened to have Momma put away in the same kind of place. I fell asleep at night praying that he didn't really mean it.

For decades, I was uncertain whether my dad's story about the CIA-led abuse foisted on psychiatric patients in Montreal, had been actual, or merely a paranoid delusion. But years later, all of my dad's sharing about Dr. Cameron was validated.

But even if the story I'd been told hadn't been true, after hearing it as a child, the world had blackened.

---

http://www.scotsman.com/lifestyle/stunning-tale-of-brainwashing-the-cia-and-an-unsuspecting-scots-researcher-1-466144

Chapter 18

After sharing my trepanning project with the class, I wandered over to the jungle gym with Nancy, who was still weirdly quiet. Nancy was my only close friend for a few reasons. For one, I couldn't make eye contact with almost anyone else at school. I felt judged, even when I wasn't. So, I was always on the alert. Most days, I day-dreamed as much as possible, staring out the classroom windows, trying to dissolve into the snow, the trees and the sky.

But also, our friendship was an easy fit because we were opposites. Nancy was the tallest student in our class, and I was the smallest. She was very outgoing, and probably liked hanging out with me because I never wanted to upstage her. And I loved that she was protective of me when kids teased. She thought that my long black super curly hair was beautiful, even though it embarrassed me, because it was totally different than everyone else's. Most of the kids at St. Basil's school had straight hair, usually blonde or maybe brown.

After school, sometimes Nancy and I would get giddy and want to put on skits for mother. I'd beg mom to watch, but she'd always tell us she had too much housework. I could tell that she was bummed out, so I'd play a kind of game with her starting with playfully pulling her into the living room by her apron.

"Okay Frances. Stop now, *bitte* – please. Momma comes," she'd sigh trying to smooth her apron.

She perched on the couch, staring at us. I knew that she wasn't really watching and that she was thinking about something else, but I liked that she was there anyway. When we ended our 'show', she'd stand and clap approximately three times, saying, "Very nice, girls!" then head to the kitchen.

But to be fair, Nancy's mother wasn't any better as an audience; she worked and wasn't home until dinnertime and by then we were toast!

Often, we would rummage through my closet and put together kooky outfits to wear for our performance. Once we wore matching pink dresses with puffy sleeves, that I inherited from my older twin sisters. Mine fit me seamlessly, but since Nancy was much taller than I was, plus her boobs were coming out, there was no way that she could zipper hers closed. I was secretly thrilled that I looked far better in mine.

Twice, I slept over at her place. We made macaroni and cheese and watched Frankenstein movies, during which she smoked cigarettes swiped from her mother. But after the second time, I decided that our sleepovers weren't worth the trouble. Each time I asked Momma for permission to stay overnight, we had an enormous blow-out.

"Why do you want to wake up in someone else's bed when you have such lovely quarters here? Ridiculous! We would never have dreamed of doing such a thing in Germany!" she'd say to me like I was out of my noodle.

Then she'd make a 'tsk-tsk-tsk' sound clicking her tongue at me. It made me huff. I couldn't tell if she was offended that I wanted to stay somewhere else, or worried about my being safe there, or both. Either way, too much of a hassle.

Sometimes in the evening, Momma let us play tag or ride bikes with the neighborhood kids. But the moment the streetlights came on she curtly called for us and we zinged home, hearts racing. All the while, I couldn't stop thinking *The Nazis might get me out here*! Sometimes that thought would hit me out of the blue, simply when I was somewhere alone in the house.

Since I got so panicky, in a way it was good that we almost never had guests over. One time, Momma hired a Polish babysitter, who petrified me. I do not know why but I could not stop crying around her.

I didn't know then about the concentration camps in Poland or how cruel so many of the Polish people had been to the Jews in their communities. But now, I wonder if my terror was because I'd somatized my parent's terror through my DNA even before my dad's disclosures had begun when I was nine? But at the same time, I thought I was insane.

Many years later, a plethora of children and grandchildren of Holocaust survivors would report similar experiences of unexplained terror, strong emotions seemingly internalized from their parents' traumatic experiences. Scientists have since proven that trauma can be genetically inherited.

Back in the schoolyard, Nancy and I sat teetering on the bars. She opened a mini package of Fig Newtons and held it out to me. I took one and opened the yogurt container that Momma had filled with a chicken neck and gizzards, which I considered to be delicacies. Feeling generous, I picked up the neck and offered it to her.

"Ugh!" she said, backing up.

I shrugged, a little hurt. I was surprised because the rare times Momma had invited her to stay for lunch, she had served Nancy and me a platter of food separated into small piles; generally combinations of cocktail wieners, radish rosettes, dumplings cut in half, olives, cheese wedges, *kishkes* – beef intestine stuffed with a combination of meat and grain, and slices of challah.

Nancy always trilled, "This is so European!"

But I was so used to dad's put downs of the food which mother cooked, that I was confused by Nancy's reaction. I couldn't tell if she was being insincere. But then she 'yummed' repeatedly while inhaling the food. It was strange that she was grossed out by the chicken neck, but I guess it was outta her comfort zone. To distract myself, I quickly moved my legs back and forth as they dangled from the monkey bars.

Other kids rarely climbed the jungle gym, because it had become shaky. Nancy and I never did acrobatics on it. We just used it to sit on. Our secret spot. She swallowed her cookie, then looked at me "Easy Frannie, this thing might go flying!"

I slowed my legs. "Woopsie. Sorry."

Then she sneered, "That trepanning or whatever thing you did for your health project was so weird in there!"

I felt like hot glue was washing over me. My guts stuck together. I couldn't move. I didn't want to breathe. When that feeling crawled inside me, I couldn't stop it.

Suddenly skittish in front of Nancy, I changed the subject and began to babble. I forced my words out, barely breathing. For a moment, I thought if I changed the subject it might help, so I gibbered on about my crush on our classmate, Ryan Arby. Nancy had heard me gush about him a lot! I waited for her to tease me about him, like usual. But she didn't.

"Okay then, let's go inside. Jumping off now!" I said to prepare her so that she could stretch her long legs down to the ground to steady herself, in case the movement I caused would shake her. "The bell's going to go any sec."

We walked inside as the bell rang. I kept my eyes peeled for Ryan. All the other students seemed to float by in a blur. We rounded the corner to our homeroom, and there stood my supreme being. "Oh my goodness, he's wearing cords!" I chirped. "He's so-o-o cute!"

Nancy smiled at him as we walked by, and he smiled back. At her! At her! Why didn't he smile at me? Did he even see me? How could Nancy smile at Ryan when she knew my true feelings?

I drew in a crisp breath. "Gotta go to the can!" I raced down the hall, then crouched in the bathroom stall chewing on my quick-bitten nails. Pain in my chest. I tried to calm down by making an origami bird from a sheet of toilet paper. My best friend was a traitor. I was garbage to her. She was willing to throw me out. Report me to the Nazis. Now I knew how dad felt about mother.

Later, at home, I ran upstairs, locked the bathroom door, and cried for a good hour. If my best friend was willing to betray me with Ryan Arby, how could I trust her ever again? Would she have me killed if she found out I was Jewish? I was pretty certain that she would have.

Momma knocked on the door. "Shnukie, Nancy is on the phone. She told me to tell you that she wants to apologize. I don't know what this is about, but I do know it sounds like a positive move."

I told Momma to tell Nancy that I didn't forgive her. After Mom left, I tiptoed to my room. I lay in bed squinting my eyes, staring at patterns on the curtains until the diamond design turned blurry and elongated. It made me feel a little better to be able to change the way things looked, as if I had some power.

That evening after sharing my upset with Diddy, he reminded me; "Your so-called friend Nancy is just like the majority of people,

Frances. They will turn you in for a few dollars if they need them badly enough." He stroked my hair, "You are a big-hearted girl, but do not be taken for a fool! I will always be here for you and you can always trust me. But only me, Frances."

I felt my body relax knowing that I could rely on Diddy no matter what. But as far as Nancy went, I refused to speak to her for weeks, and when I did it was like talking to a stranger.

Chapter 19

As close as I was to Diddy, sometimes I missed feeling warmth from Momma. What always soothed me was remembering the smell of Penaten cream and baby powder. Instantly, it was like I was back there. I could hear her singing softly as she changed my diapers. When I was upset, she was the only one who almost always calmed me, rocking me in her arms oh so gently. And sometimes she took me to a big, beautiful park near the Rideau Canal downtown, called Majors Hill. I felt so cozy when she held my hand open for pigeons to nibble the popcorn kernels in my palm under the soothing shade of trees. It tickled and made me giggle my face off. Then she'd pick me up and whirl me around, cooing even louder than the birds.

But when I was nine years old the happy moments with her became rare.

One day I came home from school and found her doing what Marcus, Sean and I had coined 'extreme cleaning'. She was scrubbing invisible spots she saw on the gleaming kitchen wall tile.

Without looking up at me she sang out: "Lovely apple slices on the counter with a few pieces of cheddar. Leave some for your brothers." I picked up one of the fruit pieces but before I could even take a bite she snapped, "Nein! No, no, no Frances! Eat over the sink like a good girl. Momma doesn't need you to make any more work for her!"

This wasn't like her. She had always been super organized but this was overkill. Bent over the sink, I chomped on the slightly brown spongey fruit and stared at the rusty faucet. Then without warning she turned the volume way up on the radio and began singing like she was angry at someone, in a very high shaky voice to an opera being broadcast.

I covered my ears. "Mother!" but she didn't even notice. I returned to my snack. She went upstairs, still warbling.

After I finished, I headed up to my room to change clothes. As I neared the top landing, I thought that I heard her weeping. I cracked open my parents' bedroom door and saw that she was at her desk, writing a letter.

I went to her. "Momma, what's wrong?" I leaned over her chair and tried to wrap her in my arms.

She stroked my arm, sighing, "Thank you Sweetheart. Life... jah!" She shook her fists. "Oych, I hate this crying! It makes my eyes all red and puffy for hours!"

"I know Momma, I have the same problem!"

She almost smiled. She looked comforted by the fact that we shared the same reaction to crying. But a second later she wagged her head and shrugged. Tears dripped down her cheeks, "Momma just needs some time."

She was slipping away from me. Was it something I did or was it her?

On Sundays, when we went to church, mom often stayed home. Diddy would grumble that she was, "out to get us". But I liked it, because mostly when we returned she'd be laughing and talking loudly on the phone in a foreign language, which I assumed was some kind of German, to one of her girlfriends who lived in another city. When she did come to church, her lips looked tightly pinched together from the moment we left the house. I secretly wished that dad would just let her stay home, happily blabbing on the phone.

But I enjoyed getting gussied up in the clothes I thought looked nice on me which Momma called my 'good' clothes and going to church. My little plastic purse contained the quarter that Diddy always told me to donate when the collection basket was passed. He usually put rolls of dollar bills wrapped with elastics in the basket. They looked way bulkier than anyone else's single bill donations.

In hindsight as an adult, I think it was his way of ensuring that we remained in favor with the priests. Little did I know then, as a nine-year-old, that things were not always what they appeared to be. And that a couple of crisp flat twenties outnumbered a roll of twenty singles no matter how fat in appearance.

The second we entered the round, brown-brick church, dad's jaw would tighten. His eyes darted around and he would give a huge fake smile to the priest. Then he'd snap at us. "Sit down in the pew and behave!"

Even though it was the norm, my stomach would always scrunch when he suddenly switched to being 'phony Diddy'. I would make myself feel better by staring super hard at the stunning stained-glass windows to try to numb myself. It helped a bit that I now got why Diddy was so edgy. He was afraid that we'd be found out as Jews. I tried to act overly calm, smiling just a little all the time, even before I did my staring at the stained-glass trick. Since he had told me who we really were, a part of me was always on guard in church, watching. And the smell of the incense, which I used to like, now made my head ache.

After church, a patient of dad's named Mrs. MacDougall – 'Call me Ally,' cough-cough – and her husband, 'Call me Jeffrey' – would often pick me up at our house after brunch and take me home with them for the day. I liked Ally's raspy voice, and warm smile. It made up for her cigarette stink. I was blown away that they wanted to be called by their first names since my parents were never okay with being addressed that casually and scolded anyone who wasn't their age who didn't call them 'Mrs' and 'Doctor'.

The MacDougall's spoiled me, and I sponged it up. But whenever they came to pick me up, I felt bad saying goodbye to Momma.

Dad told me he was sending me to be with the MacDougall's to 'keep me away from my crazy mother.'

"She forgot what Hitler did to her family!" he said, looking deep into my eyes. He took my hand. "Hitler was the most evil of men." He looked away, swallowing, "For another time, Frances."

I knew that mom was often in her own world, but crazy? She took excellent care of us. Our house was insanely clean and people often said things like how well dressed 'we Sheridans' were.

One Sunday, right after eating brunch, Momma phoned Uncle Gerd. After Marcus and Sean spoke to him, and went upstairs, I came over and sat on her lap. At some point during the conversation, she passed the receiver to me.

Dad walked by while I was on the phone and screwed his face up in disgust. It made me inhale quickly. He shouted. "Get dressed now, Frances! The MacDougalls will be here any minute. Thankfully they will take you away from your crazy mother!"

My stomach bottomed. Yet I was happy that Uncle Gerd had surely heard every word and hoped that somehow, he would find a way to protect Momma.

But this Sunday, after she quickly ended the phone conversation with him, she put her foot down. She stood up from the hallway chair that was attached to the telephone table. "Nein, Bernie! Today Frances stays home with me!"

It made me smile, but I quickly pulled the corners of my mouth down.

"How dare you!" dad growled. "I will have you put away!" My heart sped. I didn't want Momma living away from me. When the MacDougall's rang the doorbell, I remained seated next to mother.

Dad spoke to the MacDougall's outside on the front porch, and then they left. He came back inside and headed straight towards the basement without saying anything.

Then he boomed from the stairway. "You bad woman, always trying to incite me!"

Momma brushed crumbs which weren't there from the telephone table into her apron pocket, speaking in a tone which I had once heard her use to calm our cat Betsey when she tried to bite the veterinarian who was clipping her claws. "Bernie, nobody is inciting anybody. You know it would be so nice to socialize with people all together like a family–"

Diddy talked over her. "I am trying to protect our daughter from your crazy, idiotic, behavior! You put us all in danger! You have forgotten how our so-called friends, neighbors, schoolmates, and Kapos-in-the-making were more than happy to spit at us, urinate on us, while the Nazis forced us to scrub sidewalks, other things, I don't need to remind you of Liesel"

Mother covered her ears, shaking her head. She finally screamed. "Enough, Bernie! The children don't need to hear this." She stood, started to walk one way, then turned back like she wasn't sure which direction to take. "The war is o-ver! O-ver" she shouted slowly over-pronouncing each word like she was trying to staple them into Diddy's brain.

He laughed. "Such lies from you, Liesel! Don't think I don't know what you've been up to, you witch! What toxin do you put in our food, crazy woman? I had a belly ache you wouldn't believe! Frances won't be having supper here. Frances, I take you out for Chinese!"

By then I was totally confused by dad's accusations. Momma? Poisoning the food? I found that impossible to believe. But going to The Golden Palace was seriously tempting since we normally only ate there on some Sundays after church.

Comedy Club Palm Beach 2018

Y'know it's weird when people from different cultural groups who you'd never think would have a lot in common – do! – like Jews and Chinese food. Oh yeah, we go together like TV evangelists and cash solicitations. I'm sure it's in our DNA. I bet if we looked into our genealogy, we'd discover that the Red Sea we know Moses parted was red because sweet and sour sauce spilled when he parted it! That messy son-of a bitch...coulda been in my ancestor's mouth! But c'mon, any Jew knows it's a fact that if synagogues served chicken soup with sweet and sour matzo balls and bagels with moo shu chicken cream cheese they'd be packed! And not just with Jews, Chinese people would come! And what's weird is, they love MahJong as much as us Jews, so it could be followed by a tournament. Hey, we are who we are so it's ridiculous when people pretend to be something they so obviously aren't --Black people pretending to be white, Gay people pretending to be straight, or politicians pretending to be human beings. I mean d'uh! And in my case, both my parents are Jewish, but they raised me Catholic, but they were so noticeably Jewish! At church, my dad complained all through communion; (Yiddish accent) "I can't eat this cracker, it's so dry...needs a shmear of cream cheese Father, and not that low-fat *drek* – crap! But my

Dad also complained about my Jewish mother's cooking – he was an equal opportunity qvetcher I guess – but anyway bottom line - they survived the war, so food was a big deal and we always ate leftovers. I mean any freezer that contains old, withered food is gross, but *our* freezer was insane! The food had been frozen so long it changed color and shrunk so you couldn't tell what it was – it was scary looking in there, like a cryogenics lab for old food. I used to stare at the weird shapes inside plastic baggies and imagine they were tiny frozen people. Once I thought I found Jimmy Hoffa behind the *Frogurt*.

Chapter 20

Back in the dining room, I hugged Mom, who was crying nonstop, then squeezed her hand. She shook her head, dabbing her eyes with a tissue which she always kept inside one of her sleeves. She whimpered for a moment. Then she looked at me. Her eyes were so glazed it looked like she was behind a blurry window. Then she pounded the table and half-shouted, "Oh the war the war, the beautiful war!"

Every Thursday after school, mother took Marcus, Sean, and I grocery shopping at Steinbergs. I was a little surprised at how she always got so smiley when the tall, handsome store manager, who had a head twitch, greeted us. I didn't know if my brothers noticed, but I enjoyed her eye-fluttering moments. It made her look younger and happy.

"Such a nice man. Shame he has Parkinsons disease," she would say. I knew that she was trying to get us to think about his illness to cover for her flushed cheeks.

Momma was big on sampling whatever possible. She told us that fruit had been very hard to come by in Germany. The moment we got to the produce aisle she gobbled up a few berries and grapes, and any other open bin fruit like she was at a buffet. We all looked forward to the freebies.

One day, the female manager of the produce section gave her a talking to. My skin prickled. I hadn't realized we'd been stealing. But I felt somewhat better when mom puffed out her chest and said, "I'm in my right, I'm a steady customer here and I'm a doctor's wife!"

Looking back at my childhood, it was normalizing to read an article which helped make sense of my sweet mothers' behavior. Thousands of shoplifters shared the reason for their compulsive act was in reaction to a feeling that something had been taken from them which they were trying to take back. It had nothing to do with the item they stole. Many who were interviewed included the rich and famous.

For the next few weeks, she slowed her sneaky munching in the produce section. But now, my arm hair stood on end when I watched her chew or spit cherry bits into her hand. I'd vamoose into the vegetable section, far enough away to not get caught, but close enough to keep an eye on her in case she did. Occasionally, she'd waltz up to me and stuff an orange slice or a grape in between my lips, muttering "seedless" or "seeds, seeds, seeds!" It reminded me of the video we'd been shown in Biology class of a mother bird forcefully feeding her chick with food directly from her own mouth. I tried to look relaxed because whenever Momma noticed my strained expression, she'd loudly announce, "Frances, we are comple-e-etely within our rights!" making me even jumpier. Then I'd hustle farther into the next aisle, where I'd pretend to be checking out boxes of food and canned goods.

Comedy Club Palm Beach 2018

So, does anyone else beside me consider the fruit section of a grocery store your own personal buffet? But it's a teensy bit scary cuz there's always a chance you could get caught "sampling" which to be honest gives me a little adrenaline buzz. See, I don't know about you, but here in Palm Beach, the hope is to make the gossip page! I can just see the photo of me cramming my mouth full of strawberries, next to the countesses and princes they always feature – some legit, but many of those titles are bought. Well, Countess Tight-Bottom might not know who she's drinking coffee with at Starbucks on Palm Beach island right now, but 'Frannie Bananie The Fruit Bandit' will soon be legendary! It might be a tad embarrassing

http://www.oprah.com/spirit/confessions-of-a-shoplifter-reasons-people-steal/all

for the locals though cuz it's a clean neighborhood – no hookers anywhere near Worth Ave. No. We just call them trophy wives! Besides, the truth is, these days grocery store produce managers probably wouldn't give a hoo-ha if they caught me juggling coconuts naked with a banana hanging outta my ass – actually they'd probably see it as an opportunity to charge admission to the produce section, especially if I lived in Vegas.

Chapter 21

But when I was a little girl, even though dad made good money as a doctor, Momma would always bring her coupon book to Steinbergs, looking for day-old egg bread, dented cans, and other bargains. "This is perfectly good!" she'd purr, holding up a squashed coffee cake. "Smear a little butter, warm it in the oven, delicious! We could have lived on this for weeks!" I knew Momma had grown up poor in Germany, but I couldn't imagine having coffee cake for weeks on end. A cake without icing? Blech! My Viennese pastry genes ruled.

Shopping with Momma made me believe that eating and worrying went together like salt and pepper. And it made my frequent outings to cafés for pastries, with dad, even more decadent.

The last time I stood at the dessert counter with Diddy, choosing the largest slices of Black Forest cake and Linzer torte, I had noticed that his middle section had expanded. He had also grown a bushy Charlie Chaplin-style moustache. I thought he looked like a handsome cuddly walrus. But then I remembered that although he had told me that I could always trust him, he had also repeatedly said never to trust anyone else, especially not based on what they look like.

Chapter 22

"Watch it, Sweetheart!" threatened a paunchy chain-smoking cop to a boozy First Nations man wearing a cowboy hat, who had just elbowed his way through the crowd to the front of the strip club stage. I was grateful that the interaction had distracted the spectators from Boobra who had just left the stage, and was heading towards the bar, likely to berate Smiley. The doe-eyed Indian stood in front of the platform, dangerously close to the policeman, swaying. The speakers blared John Lennon singing "Give Peace A Chance" while the air stunk of cigarettes and tension. Until then, the man in blue had worn a kind smile. He was sitting so close to the stage that I could see tufts of his nostril hair, so abundant it looked like small upside-down bouquets. His nasal protrusions made me think of Diddy's unruly nose hairs, which had a soothing paternal effect on me. But his uniform made me feel both protected and nervous. My head swam with the stories I'd been told about the German police, who were Nazis.

I took a breath of hazy air and barreled ahead intoning throatily in my crisp faux British accent. "Don't misbehave gentlemen, or I'll put you over my knee!"

The cop smirked. My dark-skinned fan gave a woozy, "Wooh!" in my direction. I blew him a kiss, then turned and pirouetted across the stage several times, coming to stand near a bag of toys which I had stashed at the back. Showing the audience my behind, I bent down from the waist to access an open container of soap solution which I had pre-positioned along with a bubble blower.

At that exact moment, the Indian drunkenly sang his own version of Lennon's lyrics, "Give piece of ass a chance!" Even the cop laughed.

Borrowing from Jim Carrey, I reached through my legs (past the udder), and manipulated my butt cheeks moving them as if they were a giant mouth while I shouted, "Helloooo Everyone, hellooo!"

I heard a few chuckles. Still upside down, I reached back between my legs, dipped the wand into the soapy fluid, then flicked the stick freeing the bubble as if to imitate the release of a large fart. The audience was silent. I had been certain that the gag would generate a laugh. I repeated the action while blowing a raspberry. No response. I felt annoyed, then ridiculous. Was something wrong with me? That was so stupid! Maybe I really am crazy. Acidic juices bit my gut as I recollected feeling similarly misunderstood and unstable on my dad's fifty-ninth birthday.

Chapter 23

Diddy's reaction to the birthday present I'd given him was the total opposite to what I had expected. "What's wrong with you? You should be ashamed of yourself!" Diddy roared at me, as if I'd handed him a piece of kaka. I sucked in my breath.

That morning I had gone to Ogilvy's department store, with Marcus and Sean to spend the ten dollars which mother had given us to buy a gift for dad. I was super delighted because I found a four-by-four-inch white porcelain statue of a toilet that looked real. When I pushed its tiny gold flush-handle down the lid on the seat opened up. Out popped a little man holding a sign that said Goodbye Cruel World, which made Sean and I snicker, and after a moment, Marcus couldn't help giggling along.

Marcus said that he wasn't sure Diddy would like it. Then he remembered the silly Laughing Bag toy dad had bought and loved.

Standing in the kitchen, staring at the unread birthday card I had made, lying on the sewing table, I tried to piece together what had led up to Diddy's outburst. I remembered hearing his car pull into the driveway. I was in my bedroom, taping the gift box with lime green crepe wrapping paper. It wasn't easy trying to top it with a silver stick-on bow that wasn't sticky enough to stick anymore – Momma recycled everything.

Hoping to arrive before dad did, I raced downstairs with the present, past the open door of Momma's room where she sat studying the dictionary, to perfect her grammar. Marcus and Sean were in the living room, watching *The Waltons* on television. Marcus looked at me quickly, then looked away.

Sally was almost finished blowing up a balloon in the kitchen, leaning on the counter next to old empty Chinese food cartons that we'd brought back half full, after dad had taken Sally and I out. We'd eaten the leftovers the next day. Later, mom fished the empty cartons out of the garbage and displayed them on the counter. I thought they looked like cardboard scars.

I made it to the kitchen just as dad unlocked the back door. I started singing "Happy Birthday".

Diddy smiled tiredly. "Lovely, *meine kind* – my child, lovely. Come hug your older than yesterday Diddy."

I hugged him as the two from his "enemy side" wished him half-hearted "Happy Birthdays" from the doorway where they had come to stand.

"Thank you, I appreciate the sentiment," dad said turning his back to them. Then he whispered to me, "I set Chaplin up downstairs on the reel-to-reel before leaving for work."

I almost smiled but my head felt too hot. Dragonflies buzzed in my gut from glee sprinkled with yucky-ness at being favored.

Diddy began to sing his version of the ditty that I'd heard Charlie Chaplin sing. "Yuk, yuk sidderuk yumpona, na nee na na na nyona–"

I joined in singing and began dancing a little doh-see-doh. "… na nee, na naa, na nyona, yuk yuk sidderuk pompona!"

Then Marcus bopped in, scooping up dad's arm and twirling with him.

Sean blurted, "Where's Momma? She loves to dance."

Dad tripped. "Dancing is finished. Diddy needs to sit. Give me a minute." Out of breath, he slumped into a chair.

Marcus and Sean leaned against the counters, staring off into space. Saying something to try to make them feel better would piss Diddy off.

Dad noticed his gift but didn't mention it. I figured he sensed that I had wrapped it and didn't want to ruin the surprise. I picked it up and held it out to him, wagging it a little. "Diddy, look what we have here!"

"Oh-h-h, a surprise! Lovely, Frances – must be extra-special."

I handed him the present, gloating. He sniffed the box. "Nothing smells." He gently shook it, listening. "Very mysterious–"

He unwrapped the gift, lifting the tiny porcelain toilet out. His face was blank. "A toilet? No, can't be."

"Happy Birthday, Diddy!" I reached up and hugged him, cheek to cheek. I could smell his sweaty suit.

"A toilet?" he asked again, looking concerned or confused. I couldn't tell.

"You have to flush it to see how it works. Isn't it funny Diddy?" I bubbled.

Dad moved the tiny gold handle down, causing the teensy figure of a man with the sign to pop out. Diddy's face grew hard as he read the sign Goodbye Cruel World. For a moment he looked like he was lost. I could tell he was thinking about something dark.

Without looking at me he hissed, "You give your dad a toilet? How dare you! Did your mother put you up to this?"

I couldn't speak. I didn't know how to feel. I finally forced the words out. "No Diddy, no. We – I thought you'd really like it 'cuz – it's funny."

"Funny? A man in a toilet ending his life? You make your dad down! How dare you!"

I looked at Marcus. He jumped in. "But Diddy, Frances and I thought–"

"Your mother put you up to this!" Dad roared, scowling at Marcus.

"No Diddy, mom didn't come with us," replied Marcus.

"It's true, she didn't" I added quietly, nodding.

Diddy turned away, lost in his thoughts. He went downstairs to his study, carrying the toilet. Marcus and Sean went back to watching television. The one person who I trusted had turned on me. My insides felt hollow. I was almost nauseous. I paced. Should I call Sally? No, in a way, that would be siding against dad.

I went to the living room, and sat on the sofa, next to Sean. "Diddy's nuts!" Marcus said, flipping the channel. Sean nodded.

"No, he isn't!" I answered, snappily. "He just…got hurt."

"Whatever!" said Marcus.

I was consumed with thoughts about dad, hating myself for having hurt him. He had so much pain in him. It was the last thing he needed more of. How could I have done such a thing, thinking that it would make him happy? Maybe my brain was all messed up. That was it. I had inherited Momma's craziness.

Something hot ran through my veins. I didn't want to be put away. Panicky, I got up and headed towards the downstairs stairway. Water was running in the bathroom. I took a big breath and headed down. Even if he was going to freak at me, it would feel better than having been pushed away.

I walked into the study and sat. I re-braided my braids. Then something shiny caught my eye from inside the waste basket. The porcelain toilet was sitting on top.

I stood quickly when dad entered the library. "I'm sorry, Diddy!" I cried, throwing my arms around his neck. "I-I –"

"Sweetheart, not your fault! Diddy's okay. Sit."

I sat back down, whimpering. My neck smarted from the hour of tension.

Dad pulled his desk chair close to mine. He sat and took my hand. "Good girl. Diddy's upset but it's not your fault, Frances. I know that now."

I could feel the muscles in my neck relaxing. It was like I was an Etch-A-Sketch, which had been shaken for the past ten minutes. The solid safe feeling I always had with dad had felt as fragile as powder. Finally, now, I had my Diddy back. I was safe again. That was all that mattered.

"Frances–" he paused. "I am too exhausted to talk now. I performed two surgeries today and had a full office. I had a sandwich on the way home. We will speak in a few hours."

I knew that meant that he would wake me. But I didn't care. I no longer felt lost.

Chapter 24

As expected, dad woke me in the middle of the night. Well, I was only half-asleep, which had become my normal snoozing state since I knew that he would come to get me at some point. So, I was almost always pooped during the day.

He had moved out of the bedroom he shared with mother. The room where he slept now was called, "Diddy's room." It looked exactly the same since Sally and Madelen had moved out. Dad lay on his bed, propped up on his corduroy reading pillow. His glasses sat on the night table in between his bed and the one where I sat. I never knew exactly what he was going to talk to me about, but it was almost always one of four subjects: The Holocaust, our family, anti-Semites, or people he called "crooks". I rarely interrupted because I knew how badly he needed to talk.

"In 1913, in Vienna, when I was born, my parents, Jocheved and Israel – uch, they were so in love!" Dad clicked his tongue and shook his head. "So sweet. He would hold her under the elbow," Diddy cupped his left hand, "and lead her across the street. The paintings hanging in my office don't do them justice, Frances – I wish I had packed more photographs, but I didn't have time. I had to escape!"

Diddy paused. It gave me time to think about how much I loved those sepia-toned paintings of my grandparents. Dad hired one of his patients to make them. When I first saw the paintings, I told dad how pretty and soft-featured I thought his mother was, and how handsome his dad was, and asked him to tell me about them. But he said, "Another time, Frances. Such beautiful people, such a waste! I still don't know if they went up the chimneys or how the Nazis murdered them." He took my hand. "Enough! Let's get some soft ice cream at the Dairy Queen tomorrow. I'll pick you up after school. Better yet, hard ice cream at the Westgate Mall. Closer to home."

Mulling over whether to choose rum n' raisin or butter pecan helped me to think about something other than my grandparents' bodies burning.

Comedy Club Palm Beach 2018

It's crazy but, no matter how old you are sweets take the edge off – better than any anti-anxiety meds or even anal sex. Okay, I just said anal sex to make sure you were still paying attention. Never had it, never will. Okay maybe once but it was the west coast pot. Listen! My point is, there's a reason that in general, we Jewish people find it challenging to stay on the, 'Stop Eating When You're Full' diet and quite frankly, no matter what cultural group we belong to, we all have our naughty little indulgences. So, what's annoying is sometimes I'll be out gobbling some chocolate goody and bump into a friend who shall go unnamed and she always says something like, "Wow, Frannie, you're *always* eating chocolate! And as a friend who cares about you, I have to tell you that you're looking a lil' puffy!" So, I always continue to stuff more chocolate into my yap while answering her through a full mouth, "You're absolutely correct, I couldn't agree with you more, I have a lil' problem!" And usually, that gets rid of the problem...her. I mean it's not like chocolate is illegal! It would suck if it was – you'd probably have to buy it in some dark alleyway from the Cocoa Nostra who'd be waiting in a chocolate brown limo; the window would roll down a crack, just the size of a Snickers bar. A gravelly-voiced thug would ask "Sweedheart, whaddaya want? I gots Belgian dark with raisins, I gots some Swedish white, I even gots some strong Viennese shit with nougat – it'll fuck ya right up! But foist – ya owe us six bucks from last week!" ME "I-I'm not carrying cash. I promise I'll have it next week. Please, I need a fix today – Please, I'm so cranky and nothing helps! Have some pity – I'm hormonal!" COCOA NOSTRA "Girly, we only ask nice once!" Suddenly the window dividing the back seat slides down. Al Pacino sits there holding a giant Toblerone saying (Pacino imitation) "Say hello to my lil friend!" – I know, terrible imitation. I sound like a Jewish congested Pacino who's lactose intolerant. And I know what you're thinking - Frannie, meditation can help with stress, but let's be honest; every now and then a lil' chocolate – okay at least twice a week but there 'aint nuthin' like a tub (or two) of chocolate chip cookie dough ice cream to help me forget my childhood "Holocaust".

Chapter 25

But when I was still steeped in the horror of my childhood, sitting on the bed in dad's bedroom, he began to tell me more about my grandparents. "We were Orthodox Jews – you remember I told you about this." He glimpsed at me out of the corner of his eye. "Papa was difficult. He would get angry at me a lot, often without provocation. He had fought in the Great War. World War One, on horseback. His saber displayed on our mantelpiece. One day, I made holes in the leather couch with it. It felt good – it made a 'pop' sound when the blade perforated. He beat me terribly. I realize now he was frightened that I might have killed myself. But I was scared of him."

For a second I realized that the way granddad behaved sounded similar to Diddy.

Dad adjusted his reading pillow. "But my granddad, my dad's dad, was a rabbi who wore the long locks of the Chassidim," Diddy spiraled his index fingers in front of his ears. "Grandpa Izi was so good to me. We took long, slow walks. He taught me to recite the five Books of Moses before I could even read. I knew who I was. A Jew. I was proud. Even when the boys in the neighborhood, and later at school, would punch me, force me to crawl home through the gutter, urinating on me. I was proud to be a Jew."

My gut made noises. I wasn't hungry. I knew dad was giving me information that could help me take care of myself and our family. Plus, I could feel his ache to tell me. He didn't have anyone else. He obviously didn't trust mother. I needed to tough it out.

Dad sipped some water. "My teacher was a terrible anti-Semite. Spit in my face. Called me a 'dirty little Jew'. I was only a boy!"

he cried. "But one Gentile boy, Erich Haider, would always defend me. Many others had it so much worse! I had a loving mother, two beautiful sisters. Eva was already married living in Lodz, in Poland, Frances, with her husband and children – what the Nazis didn't do to them!" He shook his head, gulping sobs. He took a large breath and forced a smile at me. "Jah. So, I have you my beautiful daughter. Okay. So, my parents had a fabric shop – textiles. Many loyal customers, for years. Jews and Gentiles – non-Jews, Frances. Christians and so forth. We were poor, but my loving mother made beautiful food. Papa made me promise to become a doctor – so that I too could provide services for the Gentiles as well as the Jews. Jah, one day, I'm a young medical student, leaving the grounds of the University of Vienna, and I hear loud noises from the city center. I make my way there in time to see Hitler's motorcade winding through the street. There had to be thousands, Frances. Chanting, 'Death to the Jews!' over and over, Frances! A terrible sound."

I got up and sat on the edge of dad's bed and stroked his veiny hand. "Diddy, Diddy."

Diddy looked at me, but I could tell he was thinking of something else. "Was a long time ago. Thank you, Sweetheart. I tried to convince my beautiful parents and my sister Eva – she was working at a munitions factory, that we had to leave. But Papa pointed to the saber, and roared, 'I fought for Austria after all! We are safe! Don't be stupid!' Many people, Austrian-Jewish soldiers, they felt the same way. But sadly, I wasn't so stupid. Overnight Hitler took away the rights of Austrian Jews, exactly how he had in Germany. One day the Nazis barge into the medical lab at the university to beat the Jewish students, murdering many. A big burly man pounded my head repeatedly with a rock, laughing. I regained consciousness – could have been a day later, and hurried home. I was adamant to now force my family, if I had to, to leave Austria with me."

Dad opened his eyes wide and held them like that for a minute. I knew that he was trying not to cry. "I walked home – suddenly I feel the barrel of a luger gun against my neck and hear, 'Come with me, immediately!' I was certain I was dead. I am marched to an alleyway and spun around. It's Erich. Erich Haider. The boy who would protect me in school, Frances. He shows me a Death List and tells me I am on the list to be taken away the next day. That I must leave Austria immediately. I thanked him and rushed to my house and went inside. 'Momma, Papa!' Nobody answered. I go to the kitchen. Tomato sauce on the counter. No, blood. I ran out, asked the neighbors. They were taken away two days before I got there. By the Nazis. In a truck." Diddy turned to me, shaking his head at himself, scrunching his mouth. "I was one day too late, Frances. One day too late–"

Dad looked white. "Diddy, do you want to tell me the rest tomorrow?"

"Nein, nein. I'm fine."

It's like a part of him isn't with me in the room. Like he's still there. Staring at the empty house he grew up in and the bloody counter. I teeter between feeling like I'm going to burst from disgust, not being able to handle hearing a single other horrible thing, and on pins and needles dying to know what happened next.

And then dad told me how he packed a small knapsack, a photograph of his parents, and a sweater, along with a kitchen knife, a loaf of challah his mother had baked, and a small *Tanuch* – holy book, from his granddad. He headed to the bridge that led from Austria to Switzerland. The Nazis were patrolling the bridge one after another like robots. So, he hid in the bushes until the sky turned as black as he said his mother's eyes were. Then he prayed to God, peeked out to make sure that the coast was clear and ran towards the bridge. A Nazi was thirty feet away, but the Nazi's back was turned. So, Diddy crept across the bridge on his hands and knees. It squeaked with every move. The Nazi shouted 'Halt! Vart!'

"I'm not cuckoo, I don't stop," he said. "They start shooting at me 'whiz, whiz!' I can feel the wind millimeters from my cheek. But somehow, I make it over and Frances – how I survived, I have no idea!"

Dad isn't hunching his back as much, and his face is less wrinkly. I'm tangled up inside, absorbing his emotions. He keeps going.

"I am over the border, in Bethune, Switzerland. My cousins live in the northern French town called Lens, so I go there. I stay overnight. I then go to Paris where I strike up a conversation with a priest. Pere Goison. He offers me free lodging in his seminary – like a convent but for priests, Frances. A good man. But he tries to have me convert. To Catholicism. So, I tell him, 'I don't change my religion as easily as I change my shirt!'"

Dad looked at me. My brain was popping, and my heart sprinting. If Diddy had become Catholic in Paris, he would have been safe. He was really brave. So, after being beaten up in Saskatchewan, he must have felt that he had no other choice. Because it was no longer just him. By then, he had to protect our family.

He looked drained, but he sort of smiled. "Jah, Diddy has had some life, sweet girl! So, word was that thousands of German soldiers were drawing closer to France. So, I join the French army in solidarity. As a Medic. We are in Dunkirk, at The English Channel and quickly running out of supplies. The Nazis are coming down the beach, mutilating, murdering. I am trying to help. So many injured."

Dad pretended to pick up a baby. "I pick up an infant clinging to its dead mothers' breast. The milk still warm," he moaned.

I was crying too.

He wiped his nose with the sleeve of his nightshirt. "I pass the baby into the hands of another woman nearby, and at that point I decide 'I must die my own death'. I walk into the water, recite the *Shma* – the prayer before you go, Frances." Diddy looked up, "Shma Israel Adenoi Aloheinu Adenoi Ehad! And I let myself go under. And I try to drown myself."

Suddenly he looked at me as if he was surprised to see me. "Your mother – I told her this story. She was behind this flushing the toilet business, somehow. You can tell me Frances. I won't hold it against you."

"No Diddy. I told you. She didn't know. We went shopping without her."

"Okay." He nodded to himself. "I believe you. Stay here with me, we take care of each other. I will always be here for you." He fluffed his sheets. "Lie in the next bed. I made it up, already. We keep each other company. We can hold hands across the night table."

I lay down on the bed because I felt like I had to, but I was secretly fuming. I was craving my own space like crazy. My sheets and blankets. My stuffed bear. "Diddy, I'd prefer to sleep in my own bed if that's okay."

"Try this one time, Frances. If you don't like it, next time you go to your bed."

"But I–"

"Give me your hand, Frances." Annoyed, I stretched my arm across the night table. The warmth of dad's hairy hand and soft fingers calmed me down. "Sleep tight, sweet girl!" he said, yawning.

"Night Diddy!" I replied, too petered out now to feel miffed.

Comedy Club Palm Beach 2018

It's weird how the way our parents treat us as kids still affects us as grownups – and not always negatively! Cuz y'know, I'm guessing Freud would have said that my dad wanting to hold my hand at night impacted me as an adult. Like when I told my ex that our relationship would improve if we weren't always huddled together. I suggested I stay in New York and he go to Botswana! Frankly, just thinking about him exhausts me! Plus, I had the worst night sleep; Doesn't it suck when those middle of the night thoughts keep you awake --y'know, "You need to make more money" or whatever? Last night they were at me nonstop; "You are the sexiest woman and everybody wants you!" I was like SHUT-UP SHUT-UP SHUT-UP! I was awake for hours!...masturbating. Thank you...I'm so thrilled with that, partly because my ex got me a vibrator that had a rusty motor! it sounded like an angry cat! — Even when you turned it on...it sounded like it was complaining! – which sounded exactly like my ex! What's sexy about that?! So the reason I'm with my current man is he bought me a positive-talk vibrator that goes "You can do it! You're beautiful! So much good is coming!" Two seconds later I am. Hey, better to wake-up feeling bubbly instead of bitchy!

Chapter 26

The next night in my childhood home, I woke as lights flashed through my bedroom window. An ambulance siren was so loud it hurt my ears.

Sean sat up in bed. "What's going on?"

I jumped out of bed and peered out the window. The windowpane was thickly covered with ice. I ran to the door and opened it. I could feel the freezing cold draft all the way upstairs and knew that the front door was open. I heard Momma talking to a man. I couldn't hear what they were saying. I walked down the hall to dad's room. The door was open, but he wasn't there. My stomach scrunched. I raced downstairs. Momma was standing on the front porch. I caught a glimpse of Diddy lying on a gurney as a man shut the ambulance door.

"No, Diddy don't go!" I wailed trying to move past Momma.

She grabbed me by the shoulders. "Your dad is being taken to the hospital. He–"

"What's wrong with him?" I half shouted. "Is Diddy dead?"

"No. no. Your dad will likely be fine, Frances," Momma said, shutting the door. She shook her head "Jah, life!"

"Likely? What – what do you mean, likely?" I sobbed. My heart was pounding so hard I could barely breathe.

"Frances, he has kidney stones. Very, very painful. I think they caught it in time."

Diddy, please don't die! You're all I have. "You *think* they caught it in time...how do you know, Momma?"

Momma turned off the outdoor lights. "No one ever knows anything for sure, Frances." She steered me towards the staircase.

"The best thing you and I can do is go back to bed and get a decent night's sleep. One way or the other, we won't hear about your dad until the morning."

"How can you say that?"

"I am just being realistic, Frances," Momma said, half-smiling.

"Just being realistic!" I mimicked.

"Don't be fresh, Frances!" Momma said. "And keep your voice down! We don't want to wake the boys!"

I took a big breath. My heartbeat slowed and I began to shiver. I marched up the stairs. "You don't care, mother! You want Diddy to die!" I huffed.

"Such a silly thing to say, Frances," she cooed. "Calm yourself. He has really brainwashed you. Get some sleep. You deserve it!"

I stood outside dad's room for a moment. Momma went into what was now her room and shut the door. I walked down the hall to my bedroom. Sean was fast asleep. My chest hurt terribly. I couldn't get myself to lie down. I went into dad's room and closed the door. Lying back on his bed, I propped myself up with his corduroy reading pillow. His nightshirt was balled up between the sheets. I hugged it close. "Diddy, Diddy" I repeated, as if my chant might help him become well. I sniffed the flannel cloth, trying to soothe myself with his salty aroma. I spent much of the remaining night rocking myself with my makeshift dad, as my imagination wandered between visions of Nazis experimenting on him in the hospital, to his being put in a hole in the ground. 'Oh God, please make Diddy well', I repeatedly pleaded until I fell asleep from exhaustion curled in a fetal position.

Chapter 27

Still bent over onstage at the strip club, I hugged my chest to my thighs like an infant in utero. Even though my half-naked derriere was in full view of strangers, it quickly made me feel buoyant. I wanted to stay like that. Moments ago, my adrenalin had plummeted at the lack of audience reaction to my bubble blowing gag. The bad reception hit me twice as hard since the bovine G-string prop I'd revealed earlier, hadn't received a decent response either.

"Nice udder, baby, but I bet what's behind it is even nicer!" crooned one of the boys. I sighed, then looked through my legs to scrutinize my heckler. He was a male version of Betty White – in his eighties with soft puffy white hair and a kind wrinkly face. He slammed a ten-dollar bill on stage. *Bubkes* – nothing – compared to the hundreds that Boobra had engendered in three minutes.

My slight shift in position was causing pain in one foot. I unrolled myself quickly to a standing position, then spun around on my toes to face the inebriated throng. Annie Lennox's "Walking On Broken Glass" was playing. My sensitive lifted heel smarted. I was struck by the appropriateness of the lyrics.

"I concur! Shed the fuckin' udder, lady!" snorted another granddaddy-aged dude, adding a twenty- dollar contribution to my upcoming all nude debut.

"He concurs!" mimicked his friends. "We concur!" They egged each other on, attempting to entice me with additional paper money tips pushed onto the stage.

I sighed, reminding myself that I was accumulating a nice-sized cache of tips which would certainly amount to well over five hundred by the end of my shift. Plunging into a split popped open the Velcro on my G-string, driving the onlookers to a new level of frenzy. The udder hadn't popped off as I had intended but remained attached. I tugged at it but it wouldn't give. I rolled onto my back, and began waving my legs to the music, slowly working them into an upside down 'v'.

"Looks like there's a giant pink hand comin' outta your crotch!" guffawed 'male Betty White'.

"Ya get whatcha paid for, big spender!" I shot back, but my face had gone red. Spent, I lay there for a moment remembering how jazzed I'd felt transforming my old pink neon tights into the bulging prop which I'd sewn by hand. My fascination with surreal objects was birthed during childhood. Their bigger than life quality provided me with a temporary escape from the unhappiness at home.

Chapter 28

One summer when I was ten, while swimming in the river, I spotted a four-foot nail close to the bank. Wow! I had never seen a nail larger than a couple of inches. Was it from a boat? It made me believe that there was a whole other world beyond mine. Maybe I wouldn't have to be stuck in 'unhappyville' forever.

It was a few feet out from the beach. Slowly lugging it onto the shore, I wondered how to bring it home.

I managed to insert a couple inches of its pointy end through a gap in the metal bars located behind my bike seat. Holding it steady with one hand, I steered with the other as I wheeled the ten miles home.

Mother said that she was shocked that I had been able to maneuver the twenty-pound object. She referred to it as "an eyesore". But looking at it made me smile.

That winter, Sean and I built a snowman which leaned on the nail like a cane. I couldn't stop ogling it, even though my fingertips and nose ached from cold. Sean went inside. Just as he shut the door, I heard a car pull into the driveway.

"Dad!" I yelped, assuming he had come home early. I whipped to the front of the house but didn't recognize the car.

Uncle Gerd got out and shut the car door. He was wearing a dark satin beanie, shinier than the one he'd worn when I'd met him a few years earlier. He looked just as elegant as I'd remembered him to be.

"Uncle Gerd! I didn't know that you were coming to visit!" I said.

"Frances, you've grown so big!" he said warmly. "How old now?"

His accent was a lot like mom's, which instantly relaxed me, even though he was basically a stranger. "Ten. But my birthday's tomorrow!" I was proud that he could see that I was growing up.

He walked over and gave me a hug, then handed me a box of chocolates "to help you celebrate!"

Then he gave me a cardboard bakery box. "Oh-h-h, tons of dessert!" I said.

"Bartons chocolates, from New York, and sufganiyot."

"Suf-ge-what? Never heard of them, but thanks!" I said.

"Like a sugar jelly doughnut. Customary this time of the year."

I wasn't sure what he meant, so I just smiled.

"This is just a short 'hello'." He said stretching his neck. "Your mother is home, jah?"

"Come the back way so that I can show you my snowman."

I led him to my creation, which had chocolate chips for a mouth. I had snuck them out of the kitchen. Mother didn't like it when I used food for a decoration, unless it was a radish rosette which we also ate.

"Frannie, the snowman is lucky your Momma didn't use these all up when baking, or he wouldn't be able to smile!"

Just then, mom who was holding the phone with her chin, opened the kitchen window. I flinched, worried that she had spotted my theft and was about to scold me. But she didn't speak. The only thing that came out of the house was a puff of smoky air and the smell of burnt toast. She waved at us to come in.

I removed my parka and boots and edged up to the warm stove. Although she was still on the phone, now chatting in German, Mother hugged her brother Gerd. She cut the blackened parts off sliced *challah* – egg bread, shrugging at Uncle Gerd, and pointed to the receiver. She gently squeezed my arm so that I'd watch her, then tapped the ready pot of cocoa. By the time she got the mugs out I had already jumped to standing.

Watching me pour, she switched to English. "No, Bernie, Gerd is very respectful. Knows our situation, uh, to a degree. Made a surprise visit to share a little Hanukah. That's all. Leaves tomorrow to lead services in New York. Oy, what nonsense, Bernie! What was I to do, tell him to turn around and fly home?" She hung up, fuming.

Secretly, a part of me enjoyed it when mother got outraged at Diddy.

Uncle Gerd spoke to her in German, in low tones. I could tell he was trying to calm her. I almost asked Momma and Uncle Gerd what Hanukah was. But I back peddled, remembering dad's warning to only trust him and Sally with sensitive information. I made a mental note to ask him later.

I took my hot cocoa and went to the living room, where I warmed my toes on the radiator while it made cracking noises. I could hear mother speaking to my uncle. Her voice went up and down quickly, sounding almost musical and I knew she was happy. It made me like him even more.

That evening, I looked out the window, chewing my knuckles, waiting for dad to come home. The slow-falling snow soothed me somewhat. From the condescending way he had spoken about Uncle Gerd in the past, I sensed that he would act yucky about his visit. Still, I had missed him as usual, and yelped at seeing his car pull in behind Uncle Gerd's. I frantically pulled on my winter boots and parka and blasted outside.

Dad spotted me and when he grinned it felt like magical sparks flew from his mouth. "Come, give Diddy a hug!" I flew to him, knowing his squeeze was better than cotton candy. I buried my face in his pillow-y stomach, wrapped my arms around him as far as they could go, and stood on top of his shoes. When he laughed, I could hear how tired his voice was. He moved together with me, one heavy Frankensteinian step at a time, towards the back porch. "Frances, you're getting too big for this!" He glanced at Uncle Gerd's car. "Jah, our so-called guest!"

I nodded, avoiding his eyes. I dreaded what I knew was going to be a blowout. I dismounted and moved ahead of him to the back door. We entered as he shook snowflakes from his shoulders, then put his medical bag down.

"Help your old Diddy with his coat!" he said. I held onto one sleeve, and then the other, as he freed his arms. I carried the moist woolen coat to the hallway closet and hung it up. He removed his boots, then noticed Uncle Gerd's and scowled.

"Uncle Gerd made a surprise visit!" I replied, as merrily as I could muster.

"What the hell does he want?" he sniped.

He walked into the kitchen and picked up the box of chocolates that was sitting on the counter. "His kosher peace offering," Diddy murmured. I hadn't realized that the chocolates, which my uncle had also brought to us the last time he'd visited, were Jewish. I recalled that everyone, including my dad had seemed to enjoy eating them.

Dad opened the fridge and began rifling around, as I examined the box of candies. I wouldn't dare eat one before dinner, because I knew Momma would freak out. We kids' secretly referred to her as 'the kitchen Nazi'. Up until dad had told me about the Nazis, I had thought it was just another name for police. And that Nazi was spelled 'Not-See', as in "mother won't get angry if she doesn't see us swipe food from under her nose." But now, all I really cared about was how I could nab a few candies before Momma had the chance to slice each one into quarters. It was what she did with all soft candy.

"Bernie?" Uncle Gerd called, as he moseyed down the stairs. "I have made an unannounced visit!"

Diddy shut the fridge door, chewing a piece of cheese. "Jah, that's an understatement," he muttered just loudly enough for me to hear.

I hooked the swinging door that led to the dining room to the wall and scurried out the other side. Deciding to look like I was playing with dominoes, I went to our yellow and green wicker buffet, and took out a container of them. I sat at the table, far enough away not to get caught in the middle of what I knew would be fireworks between Diddy and Uncle Gerd, but close enough to watch.

Uncle Gerd walked into the kitchen, holding his arm out.

Diddy shook his hand without smiling. "Gerd!"

Uncle Gerd spoke to dad in German, then noticed me in the other room. "Hello, Frances. Your dad and I are having a small chat in German."

My chest felt warm. I smiled, and continued to watch them, even though I didn't understand.

After a couple of minutes, dad began to pace and his voice rose to shouting. Suddenly, he looked at me and then stopped. "Chocolate break, Gerd?" I saw him rifle around the box, but I didn't hear the crackle of plastic. It hit me that the box had already been opened, likely by mother. "Why she does this, I'll never know!" my dad said. "*Meshuga!* – Crazy! She knows we can afford enough chocolate for her to drown in!"

I knew then that Momma had cut up the chocolate.

Uncle Gerd stood in the doorway and shrugged, nodding towards me. "It's your Momma's way of adding even more sweetness to her life here with you!" He wandered into the dining room, offering me the opened box. "Frances?"

I eyed the bits of chocolate. Bummer! I hid my feelings. I chose a quarter of a cherry-filled. "One more," Uncle Gerd whispered, so I grabbed another piece.

Diddy continued, now speaking calmly in German. By the slow, careful way he was chewing I assumed he had also chosen a sticky caramel.

Just when it looked like they were getting along, both their voices grew loud. Then Uncle Gerd shouted, "You may want me to stay away from your family, but Liesel is my dear sister. And you are wrong to hide, Bernie! I say that again, and I stand behind it. You cannot force me to cut off ties with your family!"

Dad stormed off downstairs to his study, and Uncle Gerd went upstairs to mother. I was practically nauseous. Since we didn't have any relatives who visited us, sometimes I felt like a jigsaw puzzle which had many missing parts. But when my uncle was visiting, it was as if one of those pieces was filled in.

Just then, Marcus came through the door. I was glad that he hadn't walked in during the spat. When Diddy was angry he was usually crueler, especially to the boys.

"Where were you?" I sang to Marcus, walking into the kitchen.

"Ron's" he said. His closest friend lived on the next block. "Mm-mm-mm!" he said with a playful staccato watching me remove the top of the box. "Uncle Gerd here?"

I nodded. We shoveled two sweets each into our gullets. "Uch! Why does she have to mutilate them?" I whined, full-mouthed.

Without missing a beat, we looked at each other and mimicked mother's standard response speaking with her accent. "Because it all looks the same in your stomach!"

When dinner was ready, mother told me that Uncle Gerd had left. She sighed to herself. "Na-jah! What are you gonna do? Life is hard!"

I was bummed, but not surprised that he had chosen to go. I stood on the landing to the basement, one foot on the stairs, neither moving down or up, feeling in limbo. I wanted to go downstairs and be closer to Diddy, but I also felt pulled to stay with Momma. I called down to dad who was in his study.

"Diddy has too much work tonight, Frances. Eat without me!" he yelled. But the gross feeling in our house killed my appetite.

Chapter 29

I woke up revved to be turning eleven. Part of me wished that I was already an adult so I wouldn't have to live at home. Diddy had trapped me into spying on everyone in our family, except Sally, and then report what I found out to him. I would do things like listen in to Momma's phone conversations, and make a note of any other secret goings-on, and then tell him about it. Sometimes, there wasn't anything to share. So that he wouldn't keep bugging me for information, I would make stories up about having heard people in our family talk against him. But I didn't feel totally bad about it because the other 'side' tried to get me into trouble with mother. Occasionally, we all still felt sort of close, but we never really trusted each other. We referred to our home as the 'concentration camp'.

When we misbehaved, Momma chased us with a wooden spoon and threatened to beat us. Once in a while, I got whacked. But she often smacked the crap outta Sean and Marcus. One time, Mom beat Sean so viciously, it caused me to run down the street. I pounded on one of our neighbor's doors. Their kids attended St. Basils, too. They were Italian. Their mother gave me sugar water and their grandmother who only spoke Italian fed me pasta and said "Marone" a lot. I don't know if they had actually understood me, but the homemade spaghetti was delicious, and the attention didn't hurt either. A few months later, their children invited Sean and I over to their home. In the middle of dinner, they began to build a really cool sculpture out of gnocchi. Their mother started to beat them with her hands and wouldn't stop, even when they were screaming. It made mother's attacks seem nicer.

Afterwards, they asked me to watch TV, as if nothing bad had happened. As much as I wanted to get out of there, my breathing slowed when they turned the channel to *Happy Days*. 'The Fonz' made us laugh. Sitcoms on television about happy families, which I had started watching at Nancy's when we were still friends, like *My Three Sons* and *The Partridge Family* were a couple of my favs. Shows like *Carol Burnett*, *Ed Sullivan* and *Laugh-In* made me laugh my guts out. I never heard anyone talk about Holocaust survivors or Jews on those shows.

On the evening of my eleventh birthday, I helped Momma set forks and plates on the dining room table. Since it was my celebration day, technically I didn't have to assist, but I enjoyed placing the beautiful special occasion silverware, which had bumpy handles that looked like old peoples' twisted hands. They reminded me of the hands which belonged to eighty-year-old Mrs. Smeaton, who was one of dad's miracle patients. When she gave it to us as a present, she said "Since Dr. Sheridan cured my glaucoma, I just can't give him enough!"

It made me want to hug dad. We all adored Mrs. Smeaton's sweetness and generosity and looked forward to her company especially because we rarely had visitors. Mother served her French pastries on our good china. I enjoyed sitting close to her, listening to her shaky sweet voice. Her fuzzy grey head hair also grew all over her face. It made me think of a mother seal. I imagined that my real grandmother might have been a lot like her. Dad had told me that Momma's mother had been murdered by Nazis. When I asked him about his Momma, he always talked about how beautiful she was, and what an excellent mother she was, and then changed the subject.

I finished organizing the table. Marcus was playing "Für Elise" on the piano in the living room. Although I enjoyed tickling the ivories with him in spontaneous duets, out of all of us Sheridans, he was the one with real musical talent. When he was five years old, and I was three, we'd been asked to play a memorized duet on *The Miss Helen Show*, a version of *Romper Room*. But I wasn't nuts about the piano in the same way Marcus was. He seemed to know what the music should sound like without having to sight read. Marcus began composing original songs right off the bat and was told that he had 'perfect pitch'. So, it was really strange when right in the middle of filming, he suddenly stopped playing, stood up from the piano bench and ran off the stage. I sat staring at the television audience, lapping up the "Aw's", batting my eyelids.

In retrospect, it was my first taste of basking solo in the limelight. The feeling of bubbling adrenaline created a hunger in me for more, which would reemerge in my adult life.

At the time of the taping, we didn't own a TV. Diddy called it "the idiot box!" But he did rent one for our debut on *The Miss Helen Show*. I remember trying to understand how we could be playing piano from inside the box, while watching it at the same time, and finding it magical.

Marcus had told Momma what happened on set. While watching the rerun, she purred; "It's okay Marky, good beginning son," as Diddy glared.

"What's this, Mark? Something isn't right to behave this way, leaving your sister all alone!" dad roared.

Marcus wriggled, and hung his head. Momma stroked his head, "No big deal, Marky. Many more tries in the future! Bernie, enough!"

Diddy shook his head. I waddled over to Marcus and pecked him on the cheek, remembering how good it felt to bask in the crowd's attention.

Just as I sat down at my place at the dining room table, Momma hollered, "Turn off the lights!" from the kitchen. She called to dad who had gone downstairs, but he didn't answer. Sean, who had been fiddling with Legos at the table, hadn't left since the main course. Marcus sailed in and joined everyone who had begun to sing "Happy Birthday" to me in the sparkling glow, as mother carried a pink frosted birthday cake lit with eleven candles. Then I made a private wish that Ryan Arby would realize that he was in love with me, and dump Nancy, and then I blew all the candles out at once.

When mom turned the lights back on, I felt torn between not wanting the magical moment to be over and dying to taste my sugary cake. She came over and put her hands on the back of my chair.

"The cake is so-o-o pretty, Momma, thank you." I turned and hugged her hips, nuzzling into her tummy.

"Jah, turned out just lovely this year for my Frannie Rosie. Chocolate zucchini, can you imagine such a thing? Everybody take, take," she said.

My mouth fell open as I let go of her. Mom sat at her place and scored the cake with one hand while handing out dessert plates with the other.

"But, Mo-om, I told ya! Just plain chocolate! Why'd ya have to put zucchini in it?"

She coaxed me wobbling her voice, "Oh-h-h!" Then she clicked her tongue in the way that always annoyed me so much I wanted to run out of the room. "My poor girl is suffering so-o-o badly!" she said. "You wouldn't have known the difference had I said nothing. I had some leftover zucchini in the fridge and this was the perfect opportunity to not let it go to waste."

Dad had come back upstairs while mother and I had been talking, and set an enormous box on the buffet, making my eyes pop. Before I'd had a chance to ask him if it was a present, he sat, and began shoveling cake into his mouth like it was a race to finish it.

"Diddy, do you like the cake?" I asked, playing dirty.

"Give me a break, Frances! Stop trying to get Dad on your side." Marcus said with a full mouth.

I stuck my tongue out at Marcus, gently shaking dad's arm.

Diddy seemed to be off in another world. "Jah. Uh-h-h--Jah, zer gut. Shulenzie – Yes, very good. Sorry, I was just thinking about my sister–" Dad took my hand, his eyes puffy.

"Frances, life is precious. Do not take it for granted."

Once again, my stomach felt like someone had smashed it in. Diddy kept going. I knew that he couldn't stop his pain. "Jah, I was just thinking of my sister's beautiful little girl. She had just turned eleven too." He shook his head. "This is no coincidence that this comes to me now. Their souls are with us. You must never forget them, Frances."

"Bernie, such a thing to say on the girl's birthday!" Momma said, scraping every last tidbit of icing from her plate with a spoon.

"This is my house, and I will behave any way I choose!"

Using her index finger, mom pushed the icing off the spoon into a Tupperware container.

"But isn't you remembering right now – isn't that just a huge fluke, Diddy?" I asked, desperate to have him push away the dark yuck on my special day.

"Listen Frances, there is no such thing as fluke! They were shot, and tortured, and gassed and killed on many days. That it was or wasn't your birthday is not what matters! Don't forget, Liesel, it's not so smart sticking out your neck being a Jewish hero, teaching the children Yiddish terms and other things that will only get them into trouble."

"Bernie, it's 1972. Nobody cares if you're a Jew or a Catholic or a Druid!"

"She thinks she knows it all!" dad shouted, then nodded to the rest of us. I could tell he was trying to get us to listen extra hard so that we'd see how right he was. "Did you forget they shot Kennedy? Such a good man – for being a Catholic. And why just look at Israel, Liesel? Attacks happening daily, bombs and bullets ripping the arms and legs from the so-called chosen people!"

Momma stood. "My God, Bernie! If only we'd had an Israel to go to! My mother and my brothers, your parents and sister and everyone, might – might, have had somewhere to run to! For God's sake Bernie, we were not spared the gas chambers to adopt Hitler's religion! We are alive! We should be dancing on Hitler's grave!"

And so they were off, once again arguing about the same things, and on my birthday! This time, dad accused mother of not going to church, which he said was, "beginning to raise eyebrows with the priests, and who knows if that might make people suspicious."

"Nein, nein, nein!" Diddy shouted after Momma as she left the table. "Liesel, you are selfish! Not looking out for your family!" He shrugged at me. "How she can live with herself?" He turned to my brothers. "Boys, help me with your sister's present. Frances leave the room for a few minutes *bitte* – please, so we can set this up properly and make it more of a nice surprise, jah?"

My heart trotted as I climbed the stairs. The door to mom's room was closed, so I decided to head to my room. I couldn't stop thinking about what might be in the box. I sat gingerly on my bed. After ten minutes, I crept halfway down the stairs. One step groaned.

"Is that the birthday girl?" dad asked. "We were just going to call you."

A broadcaster's voice announced, "It's *The Ed Sullivan Show!*" followed by tinny applause.

Marcus and Sean were glued to a television which had a big silver ribbon around it tied in a bow. I practically floated into the living room. Then I realized that my stuffed pink poodle toy, Fifi-soso-lala who had been missing, stood on top of the tv.

"Fifi-soso-lala!" I squealed. "And a television, wow!"

A funny man that I later learned was named Billy Crystal was making everyone chortle. I didn't allow myself to laugh out loud, feeling like I'd done something wrong by receiving such an expensive and oversized gift.

"Happy Birthday, Frances! It's your TV, everybody knows," Diddy announced.

"I found Fifi-soso-lala in Sean's closet!" Marcus said sunnily.

Dad's smile dropped. He turned to Sean, about to freak out at him for hoarding my toy, but Sean jumped up and dashed towards the hallway. "Fuck your TV, Frances!" He mocked, already halfway up the stairs. "And fuck Fifi-soso-lala!"

I gasped so quickly it made me cough. I had never heard Sean swear and I had never heard anyone swear in front of dad. Marcus' face tightened.

"What do you mean it's my TV, Diddy?" My stomach fluttered.

"It's your birthday; I give you the television," said dad. "This must be respected by all other children as well as by your mother. Ignore Sean, your mother has brainwashed him. Any problems from anyone, let me know im-mediately! She turns your brothers' and sisters' heads. Come Frances, sit with us, we will watch the new TV; we have lots of fun! Marcus, off the couch, make room for your sister!"

"I want the floor, it's okay." I sunk onto the worn carpet. I flipped onto my side and chewed my tongue until it hurt.

Chapter 30

Rolling onto my side on the stage to face the "peeler" bar crowd, I noticed how many people were staring awkwardly. Not at me, but at the prop I'd sewn onto my undies. I forced a smile. It distracted me from feeling like a freak. I took a breath and cheated a glance at the hot pink monstrosity. Popping open the Velcro on the side of my G-string allowed the bulbous bovine eyesore to lower to the ground. Gaining full exposure, the crowd catcalled with such ferocity that my head began to throb. I pushed myself onto all fours, tossing my red mane of wig hair in a circular fashion. It felt wildly liberating. There was something in the freedom to express diverse behavior that seemed beautiful.

Standing completely naked during the applause, I almost lost my poise so suddenly that I was surprised by an odd sensation. Despite all the sexual attention from a bunch of unruly, leering men, and even in the face of my badly received gags, I was experiencing a delicious lightness. It was as if heavy layers of something other than my physical clothes had been removed.

Although I could feel the horny heat from the men as their eyeballs scoured my naked flesh like sticky, over-heated children waiting to slurp their favorite ice cream, not for one second did I worry that I was going to be inappropriately sexualized like I had been by my drama teacher from boarding school when I was fourteen. I stood on that seedy strip club stage without concern that I was going to be raped on a stranger's bed by a jazz musician from the club where I worked as an eighteen-year-old cocktail waitress after he had drugged my drink. I didn't have the slightest distress that I would be emotionally sexualized by my dad who had smeared me with a thick, inky shame which I had innocently carried forth into life. Instead, I felt safe; safer than ever. Safer naked then clothed.

So, strange as it sounds, standing in my birthday suit in front of a room full of unfamiliar and ogling people for those few moments, feeling impregnable, was deeply healing. I no longer felt ashamed. I was even moved to pick up the cow udder prop, reattach it to my G-string and tie it under my chin so that it balanced on my head like a jester's hat. Then I marched around proudly shaking my tatas, chortling at my silly solo parade. The audience rose to my level and began laughing along with me, and then applauding. When I tried to remove my pink crown, they started to chant "More, more, more!" I knew then that my shift in perspective had everything to do with their reaction.

True, I had previously uncovered other prohibited pieces of myself onstage; celebrating my once hidden religious identity as a playwright and actress and also my irreverent feminist sexual point of view as a comic, but I'd been clothed. Out of all of the emotional demons I'd confronted, due to my strict conservative upbringing, exposing my sexuality as a stripper had felt the most foreign and also the most liberating.

I stood in that grimy club, grinning. Then, for a second I turned and caught a reflection of my naked breast in the mirrored pole and without warning, my old ghost caught up to me. I flashed on a scene of Jewish women being forced to dance naked for Nazis. But it quickly dissolved as a grandmotherly type wearing construction boots yippee'd from the strip club audience and shouted, "Good job, baby. Yeah, good job!"

I picked up my bra and lassooed it in her direction, shouting "Wahooo! Women rule!"

The next thing I knew she wahoo'd back while pulling her bra out from under her flannel shirt which she then lassooed in response.

Although I enjoyed her playfulness and unorthodox maternal vibe, overall, I didn't trust older women very quickly. Momma's allegiance had often been distorted.

Comedy Club Palm Beach 2018

What's really weird is what we decide is and isn't accept-able about nudity. Ya go to the beach, where a-zillion eigh-teen-year-old girls are displaying their goodies – but if some guy walks around with like even just one of his furry boys hanging out everyone's like "Ugh! It looks like some kinda monster's living down there!" - and then the guy gets arrested! It's nuts but – yeah that wasn't intentional I'm just that in tune Baby! - but we only really want to see female fun parts 'cuz guy parts, gross us out! Listen, there's a reason 'Hooters' is a big success but not even one lousy drive-thru is called 'Testicles R Us'. Staring at a waiter with hairy ball cleavage – uch! So not appetizing! Although it would make you wanna drink more which is a market-ing plus. Sadly though, erasing that image of what'd look like two giant wrinkly oysters stuck in seaweed would require more than just martinis – you'd need a lobotomy!

Chapter 31

One spring day when I was eleven, I skipped school due to the flu, and was buried inside my comforter on the sofa, watching the movie version of *A Tale of Two Cities*. When a guillotine amputated a head, shockwaves raced through my body. Although dad had spoken to me about many murders, watching one on TV, right in front of me, felt far more real, as if the killers could come right through the screen into our living room. I thought of the Nazis and their violent killings which Diddy had told me about. I remembered seeing the disgusting statue of Jesus's crucifixion. Was that how I would die? I hadn't heard of any nice ways to die. My heart beat like a banshee. I whizzed upstairs to look for support from mother.

She was bent over the bathtub, scrubbing it like it had done something wrong to her. "Momma, Momma!" I wept. But she ignored me. "Momma-a-a!" I wailed.

Finally, she stopped cleaning and snapped. "What is it, Frances?"

I continued to sob, listing the movie bits that scared me the most. I asked her if we all had to die.

"Yes Frances, we all die!" she replied, bossily, then went back to her housework.

For a few moments, I stood frozen, too shaky inside to move. I was disturbing her and she acted as if what she was doing was far more important than my upset. It stung.

I willed myself to go my room. I lay down but terrifying images danced in my head. A little while later I went to mom again, begging her to tell me about death, but she remained icy. We had a horrible fight, during which I told her that Diddy was right. She was the enemy.

She began to cry, then blurted out "I should have had you aborted!"

Although I didn't know what it meant, I could tell by the way she instantly covered her mouth with her hand that it was very bad. I made a mental note to tell dad.

That evening, when Diddy came home, I told him that I had to speak with him immediately. We went down to his study in the basement and I shared what Momma had said. When I mentioned the word aborted, his skin seemed to turn grey. "Inhuman!" He looked away. Then got up and paced. "Inhuman!

Frances, I am so sorry you had to endure this nonsense." He came over and hugged me. I instantly felt a few notches better.

"I need to think this over, Frances. We will come up with a good solution. She needs to be kept away from you!"

Did he mean that he is going to have her put away because I told on her? No, no, no! "Diddy, she's not so bad. What does aborted mean, anyhow? I think I exaggerated–"

"Don't protect her! It's a terrible thing – you shouldn't have to know. The point is, you are too softhearted, Frances. What your mother said – she doesn't want you."

It felt like something huge had slammed into me. Diddy kept going. "Her behavior – it's for the best. Things are clear now." He headed towards the door. "I tell you Frances, I am the only one you can trust. But I promise you, I will always be here for you. Now, let's have some supper. I will have an answer about what do with your mother in a few hours."

Later that night, during our private talk in his room, dad told me that he had decided to separate me from mom. I burst into tears, certain that she was being institutionalized and that it was my fault. Even if she didn't want to be near me, I wasn't ready to lose her, or way worse, have her experimented on.

"I'm afraid you will end up cuckoo like your mother if you continue to live under the same roof, Frannie," Diddy said, offering me his linen handkerchief. "I thought it would come to this. You must always be prepared, Frances. Always have your passport ready and up to date. You never know when you will need to escape from situations. I began investigating boarding schools earlier this year. I have found you the best Anglican boarding school."

My chest was heaving. "What, just me? Where? What's Anglican?"

"Lennoxville. A small town in the Eastern townships...beautiful area in Quebec. It's called Bishop's College School. Anglican is a type of Christian. Yes, just you. For now. The others she has already pulled over to her side! Listen to me, Frances. You are a few years too young for their first-year class, so I had a talk with them. I mailed your marks, and they agreed to skip you ahead a couple of years, which will let you get a real head start on others your age! You will graduate at fifteen! But you must study hard, Frannie. That is the most important thing in this world! Nobody can take away your wisdom. I am going to send you there immediately. You'll start off in January, but you are smart enough to catch up quickly. Do not mention this to your mother!"

I felt like I was hanging upside down. I grasped for ideas. "But Diddy, I-I hated-I hated going away for more than a little while, like...when I went to Camp Katimavik. Remember?"

He waved me away. "You'll be fine. This is for your own good, Sweetheart."

How could it be for my own good if it felt so awful? At Camp Katimavik, I had hidden in my room until the counsellors forced me to get involved in activities. I was always homesick. I called home collect a few times a week. Diddy only phoned once a week, and mom as well. Dad was too busy to write me letters, and mother treated the letters which I wrote to her as if I was taking an English quiz that she was marking. Instead of sending a reply, she corrected my grammar, and sent the same letter back to me. I had felt ditched.

I tried one more ploy. "Plus, Diddy, I like St. Basil's. My marks are really good. I won the spelling bee this year."

He shrugged. "Very nice, Frannie. Listen, the teachers at the boarding school are first class. After studying there, you will win any spelling B's, C's, D's and E's! But most important, Frannie! Nothing to nobody there, ever, about being Jewish! It is very old money. Anglican. Not the type of place that openly allows Jews. Unspoken rules. I felt it."

I was trapped. Everything ached.

Dad picked up a pillow on his bed and fluffed it. "Sweetheart, go to bed now. I have to get up in a matter of a few hours."

I opened the door but didn't move. I had lost my footing. "Goodnight, Diddy." My voice cracked. "Diddy, I'd really, really, rather not go away to school!"

"Diddy knows what's best! I need to get you away from your Mother!"

"But Momma isn't–"

He came to the door and flung it wide open. I tried to speak but only a strangled sound came out of my mouth. "Frances!" He hissed. "You're acting like a crazy person, Frances! You know what happens with crazy people? They get put away! Now go to bed!"

I sucked in my breath and held it. Something was wrong with me. I was poisoned. I didn't want to feel.

Dad continued in a calmer tone. "You'll be the cream of the crop. I've thought this out very carefully. Trust me. You'll see, Frances. You'll like it! They have horseback riding. Skiing. It's beautiful up in the mountains!"

He kissed my cheek and shut his door. I stood in the dark hallway for several minutes. I convinced myself that being in an insane asylum would be far more dreadful than being stuck in a boarding school, however far away it was from dad.

Over the next few days, seeing how downhearted I was at the thought of living away from home, Diddy told me that in return for being such a big girl, he was going to take me on a trip to Vienna. I knew he thought he was giving me a treat but the thought of going there made me want to jump out of my skin. From all the stories he had told me, it felt like a seriously creepy place. That is, besides the pastries you could eat there, the opera, and the Freuds. I wondered if Nazis still lived there. I pretended to be excited because I knew he wanted me to be. We planned to leave within the next week, before I started boarding school.

When dad told mother about the trip she said, "Just Frances? None of the other children, Bernie?"

"Always wanting to start something, Liesel!" he scolded.

But I knew that mother had made a good point. And as much as I didn't enjoy being the brunt of my brothers' and sisters' jealousy, now that I was going to be sent away to school I was happy to lap up dad's affection. Everything was changing.

110

Comedy Club Palm Beach 2018

It's hard being a kid because you have to obey your parent's rules! Uch! So was anyone else kicked out of the house? I was eleven when my dad forced me to go to an Anglican boarding school which was actually a much happier place for me than my home because my folks had post-trau-matic stress disorder – which was totally understandable since they survived the war. But like Christmas gifts from them weren't very festive; one year I got pepper spray, brass knuckles and a machete! I mean, for my high school graduation present they got me a getaway car! Okay, so maybe you're thinking 'well then, boarding school doesn't sound that bad'. Uh, one lil' glitch people; See, I'm Jewish, look Jewish, and was raised by a looney-tunes paranoid Holocaust survivor who said if *anybody* found out I was Jewish they'd eliminate me. So y'know, being informed that I had to go to Anglican school was like, telling Carrot Top, right before he goes on stage; "Your audience hates redheads, prop comics, and they carry razors." And my apologies to Carrot Top who I think is a brilliant props man. I really have nothing against him personally, but I do carry a razor and prop comedy gives me the willies. I know, I know I have issues…it's because I used props when I stripped but couldn't get a laugh bent over butt naked with a rubber cow's udder hanging from my ass!

Chapter 32

I left the stage of the strip club smiling to myself like a shieldmaiden who had fought and won. My skin buzzed. I was enlivened. As the cool air began to calm my flushed skin, I headed to the bar for a celebration cocktail. The clock showed 12:30 p.m. It felt strange to want a drink this early in the day. As a newbie, I had been automatically allotted the half past noon shift.

"They hit the twin towers! Fuck, they hit the twin towers!" sounded across the bar.

For a millisecond, I assumed the men were referring to throwing dollar bills at a strippers' boobs, a game played by fashioning paper money into a paper plane. But I quickly noticed how strangely quiet the crowd had become. A throng was gathering around the television, many gape-mouthed or somberly shaking their heads. As I drew closer to the screen, I was able to take in the unfathomable destruction being broadcast on the news. It felt like someone had mushed my insides together.

A biker, a Tom Cruise-lookalike who I ended up standing next to, gagged, then quickly covered by taking a slug from his beer. He noticed me watching him. "It's a replay. Happened this morning," he said diverting attention to me.

A sixty-something bearded and spectacled man gasped, then swallowed. He quietly uttered, "Oh my god! My nephew flies for United. He's a Steward. I hope–" His voice cracked. He looked away.

Smiley glanced at him and shook his head, attempting to offer negation as a form of consolation. Nobody spoke. I wanted to hug someone, to say that everything would be okay, but didn't know that to be true.

I stayed like that for a while. After a painfully inordinate amount of silence, a 300-ish pound biker who had been standing next to the Steward's uncle loudly exclaimed, "Don't worry Sam, we'll get those fuckers! We always do!"

I was grateful for his ire as it gave me the sense that we weren't as vulnerable. But just then, as I watched the tower smoke, another plane hit the second tower.

Cries of "Oh my, God!" "No!" "Another one? Fuck!" rang out across the room. Was I having a nightmare? But it was real. The shock sunk in deeper and some of the men began to argue. I recognized it as misdirected terror. Diddy had often exhibited similar behavior.

Desperate to escape the unbearable heaviness, I fled to the second floor, to one of the bedrooms allotted to the strippers. It was reassuring to see my suitcase which I'd half unpacked. I placed a few items around for comfort. Then only removing my shoes, I flopped onto the bed. I tried to soothe myself by recalling some of the high points from my onstage experience earlier. True, I had been incrementally disappointed that my gags had taken a nosedive. But ultimately, I no longer cared about what I'd fussed over before; whether they thought I was dirty, or tainted, or crazy for working as a stripper. I knew that it was a big step towards feeling good about myself despite what anyone thought. Even Diddy. It struck me that in a sense, I was becoming his opposite. I looked forward to sharing my win with my British pal, Diana.

My hip began to smart. Luckily exhaustion won out allowing me to nap. I needed to regenerate quickly, as I was scheduled for three more dances that day.

What seemed only like moments later, although it was an hour, my tinny alarm clock fully knocked me out of dreamland. Meatloaf blared from the sound system downstairs. Not used to napping during the day and feeling discombobulated, I assumed that it was morning. Had the customers been partying all night or did this qualify as breakfast music? I glanced at the clock. It was 2:25 pm. I reset the alarm for 2:30. As I pulled my faux fur coat over my head, I felt somewhat encouraged that even in the face of terrorism, things downstairs sounded normal. I drifted back into slumber, nose deep in my fuzzy warm coat, grateful that I had it to replace the mold-scented sleeping bag. But I couldn't fall back asleep. I sat up and took another nervous peek at the clock. Only two minutes had gone by. I saw that the calendar at the bottom of my clock read 9/11/2001. Although I had committed to a six-week stripping jaunt, I longed to be performing my play. You'll be physically, as well as fiscally, fitter, I told myself. But it did nothing to cheer me up.

Moments later, the abusive-sounding alarm rang again. Still glue-like from insufficient sleep, I lurched towards the metal monster. The movement caused the shiny sleep sack underneath me to career to the edge of the bed where it teetered for a second. Another millimeter and I would have plopped onto the sad carpet, buzzing with bugs. It's a wonder that I didn't wake up before as there was definitely some kind of insect fiesta going on in the broadloom. "Uch!"

In the pursuit of reassurance, I fished a newspaper article about my play out of my purse. My play director and co-writer had encouraged me to keep the reviews with me during this tricky sojourn. "A dark and humorous, poignant, courageous, one-woman tour de force." Reading the words jazzed me and counteracted the slap of damp, frigid air. This is who I really am. An artist, I told myself over and over briskly rubbing my arms. Stripping is simply performing an audacious solo show.

I sat up, careful not to let my feet touch the ground, and slipped them into my boots, which I had prepositioned within leg-reach of the bed. Then I headed out to the balcony to escape the bug-a-thon, as the suspicious carpet squished.

I only had a few moments to ego-bathe, since I needed to hustle to be on time for my show. As I opened the balcony door, dingy air tumbled out of the room. I was certain stale cigarette smoke from the nineteenth century was still trapped inside. It was an old establishment, so not such a far-fetched thought. No time to grab a fake tan on one of the clubs tanning beds made available to strippers, so I knew I was really going to have to sell my second performance. "It's just an acting job," I told myself, trying to appease my dread.

I lathered my almost forty-year-old thighs with hemorrhoid cream to temporarily firm any dimpling, pinned the long, red, straight haired wig over my dark curls, and laid the sea green eye makeup on, Vegas style. "Hello SmartiePanties, nice to see you again," I told myself in the mirror, employing my fake British accent. "Not to worry love. Nobody has the slightest hunch that in reality you are one of the Madonnas of The Jewish Theatre." Then I pulled on my glitzy gold G-string and attached the cow udder. I looked like a confused Cross Dresser with the foreign pseudo-genitals/udder between my legs. It made me laugh. "Oh Buffalo Bullocks!" I intoned, remembering the expression my Brighton-based friend Diana had shared. I generously applied my sparkly red lipstick, doused the dark circles under my eyes with cover-up, and then powdered. I wriggled into my shiny gold push-up bra and squished my breasts as close together as the medieval cleavage contraption allowed, checking a quick glance in the mirror to relish my theatrical beauty. I delighted in how free it felt to look and act this outrageous and recalled what a contrast I was living compared to how I'd been raised. The idea of parading nude in front of a group of strangers for a few more weeks instantly felt better. I reminded myself that I had discovered great freedom in the act earlier that day. The peanut gallery no longer had the last word in determining my happiness. "I run the show now!" I thought, smiling as the reflection of the Professional Sexy character I had created smiled back. Noticing that my udder had half-fallen off, I adhered it to the Velcro. My cervical bone smarted. I had bruised myself doing the splits on stage. "That's what'cha get for being a show-off, SmartiePanties!" I cajoled myself in my fake British. "But at least now you get to decide who can peek at your..." It took me a moment to remember the British term Diana had taught me for vagina "... who gets to peek at your *quim* – vagina, and who doesn't!" I huffed, recalling the surprise unveiling foisted on me in Vienna when I was eleven.

Chapter 33

Holding dad's hand while getting off the plane in Vienna after our long overseas flight, I noticed that I had a sort of prickle in my 'private parts', as Diddy referred to them. It was an itch that burned, and it was hard not to scratch.

From inside the taxi, I could see that the city had tons of old brown and grey buildings. Dad looked around nervously. He seemed restless. I realized that it was a similar mood to how he behaved at church and I knew that he was worried about something. He asked the driver to stop at the First District.

"One minute, Frances," Diddy said getting out.

The driver was chatty. Although I loved his accent, thicker but similar to Diddy's, I was exhausted from the flight and my eyelids kept closing.

When dad got back in, he forced a smile and said, "Everything is different." He asked for us to be taken to the hotel, then turned to me and whispered. "I was at a place called *Judenplatz* – jah." He looked out the window.

The vein in his neck stood out. It always did when he was upset. I wanted to know what he was talking about, but sensed that he would crumble if I asked him questions just then.

We checked in to our cozy rooms with heavy curtains and fluffy thick comforters. The burning sensation between my legs was worse. Finally, I told Diddy about it. Immediately, he scheduled a visit to a gynecologist, my first ever, for a pap smear. He said that it was likely a yeast infection, common in girls, even babies. I had only heard yeast spoken about to do with bread and felt a little guilty. Had I given an infection to myself from eating too much egg bread? I was looking forward to having curves and everything else that might make me look grown-up instead of the flat-chested, curly-haired kid that I was. I felt almost as excited that we were going to see a "woman's doctor".

During the streetcar ride, on the way to the clinic, we drove by an enormous pillar-shaped building. It made me think of the concentration camp towers dad had told me about. I imagined Nazis pacing on its roof. I wasn't surprised when he told me that they were built by the Gestapo to protect Vienna from air raids. "To protect!" he repeated sarcastically, whispering, then exhaled quickly like he was trying to blow out bad air. "Why do they keep these 'Flak Towers' standing, Frances? Because they're proud of them. Pigs! Many old Nazis still live here, like kings and queens!" I held his hand tighter. "You see, Frances? You can trust no one but me! Nothing to nobody about being Jewish. Ever." He cupped my chin. "But you can tell me everything, Frances, but only me. Don't be bamboozled by false promises from anyone! So many shysters in the world—" He half-smiled at me "But don't worry, we will always have each other, Sweetheart." I quietly sighed with relief and snuggled closer to Diddy.

The infirmary was located at The University of Vienna. The receptionist smiled at me. Dad spoke with her for a moment in German, and then she brought me into a private change room, then left. There, a sweet-faced nurse held up a backless white hospital gown. She told me in broken English, "Take off clothes und put this on *mit* leave open at front."

"At the front." I repeated shyly.

"Jah. So, your vagina is exposed, Fraulein!" she replied.

Trembling, I wanted to take my vagina and run. Until very recently, when it had begun irritating me, I hadn't even considered it as a very significant part of my being. Then she opened a door and ordered me to, "Follow!" She walked ahead of me briskly into the examination room. "Lie down; und put limbs in stirrups, jah. This may cause some discomfort." Then she left.

After lying there for what felt like ages, with the biting feeling increasing down below, and freezing in the thin gown, a door opened. A group of white-coated adults, mostly men, walked in, speaking in German, led by what appeared to be the head honcho.

Being eleven years old, I was far too freaked out by the stirrups to do anything but stare at them. I hoped that I wasn't lying on a bed of torture.

"Guten-tag, I am Dr. Knopf," he said, smiling crisply. "You have never had P.A.P. test?"

"Um no, I- not this type of test." I gulped, looking down.

"Legs up in stirrups, jah?"

As I obeyed, the doctor, as well as about six or seven people in the group peered down and in between my legs. I couldn't speak. Then Dr. Knopf said "breathe" while at the same time sticking a cold, steel thing-y inside of me. I automatically whimpered.

He stopped moving. "You are in pain?"

"No," I sniveled.

"You will be fine," he cooed and kept looking inside of me.

"Argh!" I shouted. I didn't hurt but felt trapped.

"You have a very low pain threshold, jah?" said Dr. Knopf.

"A very low pain threshold." I automatically mimicked, mocking his Nazi-like delivery, the same way that Sean, Marcus and I did while watching *Hogan's Heroes*. Nobody laughed. I couldn't tell if he was mad or offended but I looked at the ceiling. *I'm an idiot,* I thought.

I saw him stick what looked like an over-sized Q-Tip in me. "Sample," he said matter-of-factly. He wiped it inside me making me jump. I bit my lip so I wouldn't make a sound. Then he took it out and said, "Get dressed. Results will be discussed with your parent."

I waited for a few moments after everyone left and closed the door. I didn't want any more shocks.

Then I got up and dressed.

I returned to the waiting room, where dad sat reading a newspaper. "Was everything okay, Shnukie?"

Having survived the ordeal that women went through, I felt oddly grown up. "I'm glad it's over. I didn't expect so many people to be examining me!"

Diddy stood, narrowing his eyebrows. "What? What do you mean? How many people examined you?" The other people in the waiting room were listening closely. I felt even more naked than I had been.

"Diddy, shh!"

"How many doctors were in the room?" he demanded, no quieter.

"I don't know, maybe, eight?"

Dad marched up to the receptionist, his face redder than the way my private part had looked when I'd examined it that morning, in the bathroom mirror, back at the Pension. He yelled at the receptionist, in German. She turned as pale as the walls. She handed him a paper, and a plastic bag containing a see-through container of pills.

Then, he turned to me. "Frances, come! They're exactly like they used to be – we get out of this den of low behavior!"

They? Was he alluding to the fact that the people who had looked inside my privates were Nazis?

I stood frozen. Then sauntered towards the door where Diddy was waiting for me. A moment later, my strict upbringing kicked in and I fidgeted, feeling impolite leaving with such bad manners. Dad held the door open. He turned back towards the infirmary and shouted, "You should be ashamed of yourselves. She's a virgin!"

Every bit of my body clenched down to my baby toe. A young couple moved past us quickly to enter as he continued to yell, "Training class of students! The nerve! I needed to sign a release. Illegal! They think they're dealing with a Moron. I let her have it."

Dad took my hand and wordlessly hustled me into the university courtyard. After a few moments I felt his hand relax. "Just a little infection as I had hoped. Urinary tract. When germs called bacteria get into the urinary tract, they can cause an infection. But you can never be sure. Always a good idea to be checked out!" He held up the bag "Antibiotics. They had a sample."

As I wondered why he had hoped for a urinary tract infection he said, "I was worried it might be something worse. Thank God! I would die if anything happened to you. I don't even want to think about it!"

"I'm perfectly fine, Diddy," I said, squeezing his hand. I cheated a glance and saw that his eyes were wet.

Then dad took me on a tour of the medical school grounds to show me where he had studied. Pointing to a bench he said, "Jah – this is where–" he shook his head, "that monster decided to make an example of me. Terrible, a Nazi, a real murderer. If it wasn't for my friend Erich Haider–"

I gulped, remembering the story dad told me about how his friend had leaked to him that he was on the schedule to be captured. It had given Dad time to escape. What if he hadn't? He could have easily died in a concentration camp like so many people in his family. I noticed that I was breathing fast. I shook my head. It was too much to even think of it. As if Diddy could tell that I was upset, he took my hand. "Come dear, let's think good thoughts."

By the time we got on a streetcar, I was feeling much better. We took it to the opera house in the center of Vienna and walked a bit. Proudly smiling, Diddy stopped in front of a heavy white carved hotel door.

"I am taking you for the most famous chocolate cake in the world! Sacher torte."

"Grea-a-at! Oh, this is Hotel Sacher. Got it."

For years, dad boasted about the hotel and its yummy cake. We entered a dining room. It had marble walls and crystal chandeliers. The hostess wore a tiny strand of pearls and a velvet jacket. She had the same curled bob hairdo as Edith Bunker from *All in The Family*. She nodded at us, fake-smiling. Dad spoke to her in his, "I want you to like me" tone. She showed us to a small oval marble table. Moments later a waiter wearing white gloves brought us ice water with two *kaffee mit shlag* – strong coffee topped with fresh whipped cream. I couldn't stop smiling.

Diddy handed me two pills. "Swallow, with a gulp of water."

I took the antibiotics. A moment later, the waiter returned, and placed a wooden box with a gold latch in front of me. It reminded me of Momma's green leather-covered jewelry box, which also had a gold latch, and the hours I'd spent carefully examining her collection.

"Diddy, wow! A jewelry box?"

"Nein. Open it and you will see."

Inside the pine box was a dry-looking iced chocolate cake, with a teensy layer of jam and a thin chocolate medallion on top. I was puzzled how such an elegantly displayed treat could contain such a yucky-looking chocolate dessert. "Wow! A cake!" I said pretending to be pleased. Realizing the dried-out loaf would require moistening, I took a gulp of coffee before eating a bite. Wet, it tasted like apricots and mocha, far from horrible.

I stalled before saying anything about it, fantasizing about pouring my coffee directly on top of it and mixing it in the box. It struck me that the Hotel Sacher's torte had looked far better in the box, from the outside, just like a few other things in Vienna thus far. Dad had promised that the University of Vienna clinic "treated patients with the utmost respect." Nope. And that morning, while we ate breakfast in the plush, curtained, dining room at the Pension, dad eavesdropped on the handsome Viennese owner as he spoke to a man who was staying in a room down the hall from us. "Nazis!" Diddy whispered to me.

"You are taking time to enjoy every morsel!" Dad said, happily licking the side of his fork.

Faking it, I "yummed" all the way to the last bite of my slice.

"Keep the box as a nice memory," he said, handing it to me as he paid the bill. I smiled back at him.

Dad took me to the opera, to the best schnitzel restaurant, and to Salzburg to see the giant marionettes who danced to Mozart. He took me on sightseeing walks through his old neighborhood on Grundsteingasse. At one point he stopped at number three Weyprechtgasse and stared across the street at a small building. He spoke slowly, thinking, blinking tears. "That was my home. Bombed by the Nazis. Now a dry cleaner. Jah, what you gonna do!" He took my hand and walked. I knew that he was trying to stop being upset. It felt like we were in a creepy fairytale.

The next morning back at the Pension, I noticed him looking out the window, humming to himself. I guessed that he was enjoying happy memories he'd experienced somewhere nearby. Then he bought a Euro-pass for the train and took me to Paris. We were greeted at the station by a smiling man wearing a beret, who he introduced as Pere Goison. I recognized his name, as the priest who had sheltered dad from the Nazis and tried to get him to convert. They kissed each other's cheeks and spoke quickly in French. My chest felt warmed by the sweetness between them.

Diddy introduced me, cupping my chin with his hand, showing me off.

In retrospect as an adult, I concluded that my dad's emotionality must have been a reaction to this being the first time they'd seen each other since the war. Being able to parade his offspring was a testament to having triumphed against the Nazis.

We headed to the station café as they rattled on in French. I only understood the occasional word. I was satisfied to read the exotic menu in between studying my dark-haired reflection in the stunning mirrored walls.

When the waiter appeared, dad asked me, *"Veux-tu du lait?"*– Would you like some milk?

I automatically answered in English. "Yes please."

Diddy slapped the table causing me to go "Wooh!"

"En Francais!" he barked. I hung my head and said nothing. I hadn't expected him to want me to speak French. *Why is he being so mean? He never forced me speak French before.*

"Encore! En Francais!" Again! In French! He practically growled.

My bowels churned. I raised my head, piecing together the French I remembered. *"Un verre du lait sil vous plait?"* – A glass of milk please? I asked the impatiently nodding waiter.

Pere Goison said something to dad. I was relieved that it seemed to soothe him. The priest removed his beret, and stroked my arm, asking me about myself in broken English. I tried to answer him but I was forcing down sobs so hard, my head ached.

Later that day, I silently forgave dad while the saleslady in a boutique on Rue du Printemps "Ooh-la-la'd!" over me. Diddy was having me outfitted for a green leather jacket. I had never had such a grownup coat. It felt soft, and looked fancy. Its emerald color made the green flecks in my hazel eyes pop.

That night, we slept at the home for priests. I heard people walking on the floor above us and couldn't sleep. I gazed out into the courtyard, imagining Nazis lining up the Jews.

In the morning we ate breakfast with the Fathers at a long table. Dad was joking with them in French and they were all laughing loudly. They gave me a hunk of French bread swimming in a bowl of milk. I took a bite. It made me gag. Diddy's face grew red. "Don't be fresh Frances, or I'll give you such a slap!" I could feel how ashamed he was of me.

I hung my head and took small bites. I was shocked at dad's treatment of me and couldn't understand why.

Later, I asked him what they had been laughing about. He told me that the priests had been telling what he called dirty jokes. I felt nauseous just like I had when he had spoken to me about washing his personal parts.

Comedy Club Palm Beach 2018

Ladies and Gentlemen, we have a special guest this evening...a Stripper! Let's clap it up for 'SmartiePanties'! (Frannie does a 360) Tada! Sadly, I was fired from my last stripping job because I'm dyslexic which really pissed off my boss 'cuz – I threw money AT the crowd. Yeah, first I'd get on stage completely naked, then get dressed and jump IN-to a cake. Anyway, friends sometimes ask if I was frightened the first time I stripped, y'know fully naked in front of a crowd. Please, I was already a pro at eleven. Okay, I'm spread out on a gurney in Vienna, buck naked with my legs in stirrups like an upside-down Lady Godiva, while this doctor and seven students stare at my knish like they were Mormons who'd just discovered where Joseph Smith had hidden the golden tablets! Then they whisper to each other in German, and my German's not great but I'm pretty sure they said (German accent) "Somevun should call Heinrich za janitor. He'd get a good laugh out of zis!" So then, the doctor inserts a swab into my y'know – shmengypoopen – that's Latin for vagina, and they murmur excitedly like they're saying (German accent) "Oh zis is our favorite part vere he pushes it in too far and has to put on his miner's helmet and go in after it."

So, do I get nervous dancing from the safety of the stage in front of a bunch of half-drunk old guys who probably couldn't remember the last time they had sex that didn't involve some woman sitting on their lap for $20? Nah, not really.

Chapter 34

Rummaging through my suitcase in the hotel room above the strip club, I reveled in how I had rebuilt my emotional footing in the six weeks since I'd begun working as a dancer. Every single time I had gotten naked onstage had been worth it, even while weathering pole burn. Before I climbed the stairs leading to the stage, I would zero-in on the feeling of innocence and communion I'd felt with others, that first time I'd removed all my clothing publicly. As a result, I was having a pretty consistently great time, whether my onstage clowning received approval or not.

Then, I trained myself to zoom in on feeling that good in every circumstance. I made lists of things that made me happy and day-dreamed about them. It jazzed me while I fraternized with other strippers, when I was alone in my room – even kibitzing – chatting with Smiley was now mostly fun. But when it wasn't, I just ignored him or secretly thought the words "bla-bla-bla-bla-bla" while he complained.

I knew that I was essentially re-brainwashing myself, and although I didn't always reach a state of bliss, I felt a helluva lot better. Even my digestion improved significantly. And I was able to view my past through a softer lens. Recalling sad events was easier since I now knew how to counter them.

Over the years, I had wondered why dad had been so tense when he had taken me to the seminary in Paris. Now it hit me! He had desperately wanted to blend with the priests, but didn't. He had felt like a phony and they sensed it. They knew that he had converted out of fear. After all, in 1940 he had told Pere Goison, "I don't change my religion as easily as I change my shirt!"

Diddy had attempted to show the priests that he had left the persona of Bernie Sigal behind to become Bernie Sheridan, an entirely different, happily Catholic man. But since his conversion, had he secretly felt split in two?

I shivered, but it wasn't only due to my feelings. I hadn't been able to get warm for a single moment in the icy hotel room where I'd slept during my stripping escapade. Cupping my nose, I attempted to warm it by breathing warm air into my hand. Although I was already wearing a sweat-shirt and wool hat, I wriggled into a sweater I'd brought, a purple athletic cardigan leftover from boarding school. It fit like a wool condom. I could hardly move my arms. But I was amazed that I could squeeze into it at all, considering I'd worn it from the age of eleven, the year dad first brought me to Bishop's College School.

Chapter 35

After two weeks in Europe with Diddy, we flew back to Canada and landed in Montreal. He rented a car and drove us through the Laurentian mountains towards the boarding school. They reminded me of the foothills in the Austrian Tyrol which we'd visited for a day.

Although he was forging a hard smile, he almost sang, "Look around, Frannie. Beautiful!" like we were going on a second vacation.

All I could think was, *I can't believe you're really going to leave me here.*

Diddy patted my leg, "Shnukie, you will be just fine. You have a chance, now that I got you away from your crazy mother!"

He's right. Momma is crazy, I had tried to convince myself, but I didn't believe it. We'd left without telling her. Dad had allowed me to phone her from Vienna, but made me promise, again and again, not to tell her how long we were staying away. "Not one word, not a single word about school to your mother, Frances!"

When she asked questions, I'd reply like a robot saying what he had programmed me to, "Diddy said to ask him directly."

"Put your dad on the phone," she'd demanded once.

"He's not here right now," I had been instructed to reply, and did.

Momma went silent. "Be safe, my angel," she finally said. "I love you."

Careful not to let Diddy hear, I whispered, "You too."

After a couple hours in the car, dad pulled into the school's entrance. Its grounds were made up of rolling snow-covered hills and frosted trees straight out of a winter-land fairytale. We drove by a number of old dark brick buildings which he said were called 'Victorian'. He stroked my head, "You'll make some nice friends here, you'll see."

"But Diddy I–" I began to protest but then seized up, unable to finish my sentence. Instead, a loud twisted sound emerged from somewhere deep inside "Anhhh!"

Dad slowed the car, looking at me with disdain. "How dare you make these crazy sounds? You're not normal! You know what happens with crazy people? We have them put away! Pull yourself together by the bootstraps and behave! You have no idea how good you'll have it here."

I looked away, gutted. I peeked at Diddy while repeatedly thinking what he'd stuck in my brain *You're the only person I completely trust* hoping that he would hear it somehow and realize that the right thing to do was take me back with him. But nothing changed.

We arrived at the dormitory that he said I was going to be living in. A bald, pigeon-toed man who had buggy eyes came to meet us. He shook dad's hand and said that he was my housemaster, Mr. Ketchen. Diddy trailed us as Mr. Ketchen showed me to my room.

He turned to dad without smiling, "Dr. Sheridan, although you're two days early, we will make meals available for Frances."

Diddy thanked him but I was fuming inside. I could have spent more time at home.

Dad and I went outside and finished unpacking the car. He gave me fifty dollars and told me he would send more. I felt dazed. "You are in time for supper. Go to Mr. Ketchen and ask directions to the food hall. I'll get going now, Frannie" he said looking away. "You phone me every day. Study hard. Really crack down and you will succeed. And don't let any fresh boy touch you. If you are scared, you yell 'Help'! Loud!"

He turned to me. His eyes looked tired and sad. He re-opened his wallet and handed me a few twenty-dollar bills. "Extra, in case of emergency. Put quickly in your wallet." He hugged me good-bye. "Remember Frannie, nothing to nobody about anything Jewish. It could cost your life. People pretend to be a friend, and talk behind your back, I could tell you stories. You are a very sweet, soft-hearted girl, don't be taken. People will swindle you at the first chance you give them. Be well behaved or you will be responsible for dangers that will come your way. Remember Frannie, I am the only person that you can trust!"

For a moment, I was able to hang on to the thought that I could trust Diddy, because I certainly didn't trust myself. I had Momma's crazy genes, after all. But then he drove away, waving. The car rounded the corner. It felt like my veins were boiling. I raced after it, screaming, "Diddy wait, Diddy!"

He kept driving. My body felt like it was crashing in on itself. I kept running after the car for a moment or two, even though it was now speeding away. I crouched at the side of the road, collapsed with sobs. Then I stayed as still as I could, breathing shallowly, hoping to make myself disappear. I could see my breath in the freezing air, and I could hear my heartbeat. Not a single soul was around. I stayed there until the sun set.

The semi-darkness made me feel like I could hide a little. Willing myself to stand, I then walked to my dorm room. I caught my reflection in a mirror. My nose was red just like Momma's got, making me miss her.

Just then, the wind blew through the trees causing a branch to knock the window. *Was Momma thinking about me?*

Exhausted, I fell asleep on top of my suitcases on my new bed.

The next day I woke up with a sore throat. Mr. Ketchen met me in the hallway. He sent me to the infirmary, which smelled like cookies, and where I met an overweight nurse named Miss McNab. She had chocolate dots around her mouth. Even though I knew that she hadn't put them there on purpose, I thought they were a nice contrast to her white nurse's dress. While she examined me, I was awe-struck by her green eyes. Her pupils were vertical, like a cat. I wondered what Diddy would have thought of them.

She handed me a bottle of cough syrup that she said contained codeine. "Take it when needed."

I headed back to my room, unscrewed the cap and took a slug. The sugary sting was delicious and made me feel warm and relaxed. Without realizing it, I drank practically the whole thing and fell asleep again on top of my suitcases. I woke up, fuzzy as Mr. Ketchen knocked. "Frances, you're going to miss dinner!"

"Just having a nap, Mr. Ketchen," I found myself slurring a little.

"You have to attend meals! Report to the Dining Hall in half an hour sharp! Understand, Frances?"

"Yes, Sir."

He shouted the directions through the door. Then I listened to his sloppy footsteps retreat. I unpacked some toiletries, opened the door and located the bathroom.

I decided to head outside. I peeked into the hall to make sure he hadn't returned. Then, I hustled towards the front door noticing a sign on the wall which read Gillard House.

As I walked out of the dorm the evening air soothed my codeine-buzzy skin. My flesh felt prickly, just like my mouth did after the dentist had filled a cavity and I could feel the anesthesia wearing off. I was surprised that I wasn't hungry. Instead, I was craving more of the sleepy, buzzy feeling from the cough syrup, so I headed back towards the infirmary.

I passed two sports fields, which were bordered by a thick forest. While remembering Diddy's stories about the Jewish partisans who hid in the woods and fought the Nazis, the gnarled trees held me in their spell. I knocked at the infirmary, forcing my cough as Mrs. McNab, opened the door. The TV was on.

"Yes! What can I do for you, Frances?" she snapped, keeping her eye on the television.

I coughed even more dramatically. "My throat is absolutely killing me and I finished the bottle!"

"Come in then," she sighed. The place smelled like pizza mixed with antiseptic.

"That went fast. I guess you needed it. I'll be back."

She returned, handing me another, much bigger bottle of the same syrup. "This should do the trick.

Let me know if you need more."

I took it to my room, drank half the bottle, and fell asleep.

My eyes were still closed when I heard muted voices outside my window. I pushed a suitcase off the bed onto the floor and sat up in its spot. I peeked outside. The sunlight hurt my eyes. A bus was parked outside and students were bringing suitcases into the dorm. I heard people in the hallway walking by my room to theirs.

I noticed a slip of paper under the door. I picked it up, opened it and read: Miss Sheridan. You are required to sign in for every meal, or further disciplinary action will be taken.

Before I had time to think about it someone knocked, then opened the door so quickly I had to jump back to avoid getting hit. A muscly girl with waist-length dirty-blonde hair wearing a 'Candy is Dandy but Sex Won't Rot Your Teeth' t-shirt, and skin-tight blue Levis asked "This 4A right?"

At first, I thought she was at the wrong room, because she seemed to be a few years older than I was. Then I remembered that I was advancing two levels.

"Yes," I replied.

"Looks like we're roomies!" She carried a soft-looking gold leather shoulder bag and wheeled a gigantic matching suitcase into the room. My neck stiffened like fresh taffy on snow.

"I'm Jackie. What's your name?"

"Frannie. Nice to meet you," I said jittery.

"So, do you definitely want that side? I mean, it would be nice to toss a coin."

"Side? Of the room?" My voice sounded hoarse and it felt like my body was being pressed inside itself. *Are there sides here too?*

"Duh! What did'ya think I was talking about?" She tossed her mane of hair forward over her head and back, and made it look fluffy.

I stopped myself from breathing for a few seconds. Had I revealed an awful piece of information about my family, which was split into sides? "Oh, sorry," I said, when I realized what she meant. "Would you prefer this one?"

"Yeah, if that's cool. I have a right-side thing." She dragged my suitcase that was on the floor over to the other side of the room and pushed hers next to the bed I was perched atop. I couldn't stop staring at her luxurious luggage.

"School sucks, eh?"

I nodded. "Your luggage is gorgeous!"

"Italian! I like Italian things."

"Is there a small Italian in your suitcase? It's big enough!" I found myself joking, then gasped. "Not that my family's tall or anything, believe me!"

Jackie laughed.

"Okay. Gotta go to the bathroom." I darted to the bathroom. While talking with Jackie, I had urinated on myself. I locked myself in a stall and stayed there for forty minutes making abstract origami from a sheet of toilet paper.

Over time I relaxed somewhat around Jackie. But it felt like my body would dance with sparks when I was around everyone else. My hormones bubbled around boys, but I was terrified of speaking to a 'dirty boy'. Jackie thought I was just being shy and tried to cheer me on. I would think about the words over and over, missing the opportunity to interject, my stomach tightening, certain that whatever I said would be ridiculous, coming from a nut case.

Often, I would find somewhere to hide and then practice what had occasionally worked to soothe me at home; over-focusing on an object like the stunning dark wood décor of the Victorian school walls, trying to lose myself in it to stop myself from feeling bad. I attended classes just enough to pass.

Jackie and I had occasional giggling fits. But my laughter was such a gigantic release from the tension which almost always seemed to be with me that it caused me to pee through my clothes. Once, during a dorm house meeting, Mr. Ketchen tripped while he was pacing in front of the room. I laughed and peed so hard that I refused to leave after the meeting had ended, telling everyone I was feeling nauseous and just needed to sit and breathe, because I knew that I had left a wet spot on the furniture.

I thought about calling mom, but I didn't trust that she wouldn't tell dad who continued to warn me not to, during his daily phone calls. He said that if I did, she'd make me come home and then I'd end up crazy like her. I told him that I found school difficult, but he said that was good. That if I kept my nose in the books I would succeed. I was certain that if I told him about my panic attacks he'd have me "put away."

Over the year, I found every excuse to need more cough syrup, which was always available. I fell into a routine of drinking after Jackie was asleep, and then woozy, I'd sneak outside. The dark woods called to me, even though I'd see large dark shadows of animals and even come face to face with the occasional fox or raccoon, and especially whenever I came upon an opening in the dark cover of branches and a sudden enormous smattering of stars.

Comedy Club Palm Beach 2018

Any campers in the crowd, people who like to get out of the city? It's weird but d'ya ever wonder why it's so calming to be out in the country? It's because animals rarely complain. Well, unless they're around tofu-eating vegetarians. You'd think animals would appreciate being spared and respect a vegetarian menu but no, even raccoons going through their garbage and hitting on some tofu are like (spit)"Who eats this shit! Those humans are so stupid – hey humans! Y'know why they call it tofu? 'Cuz it stands for 'throw out fucking useless!' Have some pride people – we're animals, but you don't see us eating sponges!"

But even with the psychological abuse from animals, being in nature for us humans is a nice break from hanging out with stressed-out people downtown. Like my nephew works at Starbucks in the city, and I asked him how he handles the stress and he was like, "It's easy! When customers piss me off, I serve them decaf!" And then, he always makes sure the lid looks like it's on securely...but it never is.

Uch qvetchy people – and it's contagious! Listen to me, I'm qvetching about people qvetching which makes me qvetchier than the rest of them! But luckily, I found yoga and it really helps me chill out! Any yoga people here? You're probably familiar with Downward Dog, and the one-legged Prayer Position...well I created what I call 'The Ostrich'. So like if you're in line at Starbucks and the person behind you goes "Uch, this is taking sooo looong!" Just do The Ostrich! *Bend your elbows and move them like wings, while aggressively clearing the phlegm from your throat and then kick ninety degrees behind you. Never actually make contact*. Then say "Woops! Too much yoga...too much caffeine? Namaste(wink)."

Listen, I'd never kick anyone – I'm originally Canadian. But I thought about it so, beware cranky people...'cuz, I do have dual citizenship.

Chapter 36

I went home for a long weekend, heart leaping. Momma hugged me for what felt like five minutes, and I let it go on. She told me that she knew dad had forced me to keep things secret, but that she had been crazed with worry.

"I missed you, my Sugarplum," she said using her signature endearment for me. She stroked my cheek. "I know your dad fills your head with lies, insinuating that I am crazy. Maybe I am," she shrugged. "Who wouldn't be after living with him?" she added, laughing. "Frances, he needs serious help.

As long as you are happy where you are, Momma is happy."

I held her, burrowing my face into her sweater, relieved that she didn't blame me.

As soon as he saw me, Sean hugged me harder than ever, but then realizing how closely we were standing, became a little frosty. Marcus said he'd missed me and asked me all about school. I had expected them to tease me about being favored, sent to a private school, but they didn't.

Back at school, Dad repeatedly interrogated me to make certain that I hadn't divulged our Jewishness.

Most nights I continued to sneak out, too dark to even see my shadow, walking for codeine-hazy hours in the icy mountain air.

The only time I felt almost okay in public was during athletics – soccer, ice-skating, field hockey and track and field which required so much focus on physical alignment, that I automatically forgot to feel bad.

After my first long weekend, I didn't see mother again until Easter, and then only for half a day.

Diddy arranged for me to spend all future holidays at the homes of some of the other girls who lived in my dorm. When I asked him if I could come home instead, he always warned that if I did, I'd end up cracked like Momma, so I stopped trying.

During my last year, when I was fifteen, I took solace in reading everything I could get my hands on, including the dictionary. It felt like warm cocoa was running through my veins knowing that I was imitating Momma's behavior.

That year, mom phoned me at boarding school for the first time. I used big words, trying to impress her, but the first thing she said was "Frances, I'm leaving your dad."

As the seams that held me together fell away, I begged her to stay at home. She said that Sean was going to attend private school, and Marcus was going to live with her. He had been sent to a private school the previous year but was unable to cope and had been living at home, acting strangely. She refused to give me details, diverting the conversation by trying to lift me with; "Sugarplum, I'm not leaving you. I never will. Just Diddy."

By the time I went home for the final time, Momma had already left. Almost everything had been sold. The house looked as disemboweled as it felt without her there. I wandered in and out of the empty rooms.

One square area on the wooden floor of Marcus's room was shiny, wax still intact. I smiled recalling that his night table had stood in that spot stashed full of humor magazines I loved to read. The carpeting in the room I'd shared with Sean held eight small round grooves in the shape of the feet from our two beds. It struck me that whether an object was inanimate or animate it could only bear immense pressure for so long without negative consequences.

I turned away and walked into Diddy's room. He had packed a steamer trunk next to the two beds. I wasn't looking forward to sleeping in that oppressive environment again, but it was only one night. I mused that since Momma wasn't physically in the house any longer, hopefully his need to talk about her disparagingly would be lessened. Holocaust stories were somehow easier for me to stomach.

I dawdled towards Momma's empty bedroom, but unexpectedly a small sob escaped from my throat, stopping me. I took a couple of calming breaths hoping that Diddy hadn't heard, then headed down the stairs. I knew their every creak, and the feel of each worn step. It cheered me a little that at least nothing had changed there.

Upon entering the kitchen, Dad handed me a plate of radish sandwiches. "Good timing! Not much in the fridge, but have a snack, jah?"

"Thanks Dad," I said feigning interest. I wasn't hungry.

"Good," he said chewing characteristically open-mouthed. "Crunchy!"

Annoyed, I took the smallest nibble possible. Luckily, he was too involved in attacking his food to notice.

On the morning of my return to boarding school, I felt lighter, happy to be leaving the broken nest. But by afternoon melancholy caught up. It was disorienting not knowing where my home base was anymore. I felt rudderless.

Dad sold our home, retired and moved to Vienna, where he lived as a Catholic. My grades continued to drop. He was advised of my misbehavior but could do very little to discipline me all the way from Vienna. He gave me a talking to on the phone about acting like a crazy person, and wrote me a surly letter, hoping it would make me step back in line. He fervently warned me, "Never tell anyone that you're Jewish!"

I continued to drink cough syrup every night and read and write in my journal during the day. My pretty English teacher, Ms. Burke who sported a dark curly afro, lived in an apartment connected to our dormitory. She had always lauded the essays I'd written.

One day during drama class which was taught by an animated man named Mr. French, I found myself standing offstage in the darkened auditorium, waiting for a cue. It was the first time that we had acted out scenes. Food came up into my throat. I swallowed it back down, hearing Mr. French say, "Frances, go stand in your light."

I moved into a large spotlight.

"Begin!" he said.

I began to read Juliet's lines from Romeo and Juliet. Until that very moment, I had felt like I was a snow globe which someone else continually shook, but the moment I spoke the words of a character, everything settled.

Then, Mr. French said, "Jean, go!" At which point, my classmate, Jean, began reading Romeo's lines.

I bubbled in the alchemy of holding the class's attention, speaking the words which belonged to a character, with ease. Mr. French commended my ability. I decided to pursue a theater degree.

Then, Mr. French. said "Frannie and Jean, I want to work with you."

He brought us to a space behind the auditorium and told us to lie down facing each other. A technician was fiddling with some blue-colored stage lights.

"Now, push your bellies together and allow the warm loving feelings to flow between you," Mr. French commanded.

My body stiffened. I emitted a small sound, then quickly quieted myself. I looked at Jean, but he averted his eyes. The technician left.

"Frances! Jean! Move together! Now!"

Without looking, we pushed against each other. Mr. French watched for a few minutes. "That is what you need to feel during the scene," he said.

Almost on cue, the lights changed to a yellow-green vomit color. I recognized that it was similar in color to the light I'd seen in Diddy's room, the night he'd first started telling me stories about the Holocaust.

Mr. French watched as Jean and I got up without looking at each other as we went our separate ways.

That evening, I went to Ms. Burke's apartment to tell her what had occurred. She immediately went to confront Mr. French.

Afterwards, she told me that he had been entirely inappropriate and was lucky I didn't want to sue him. Then she took me to have my long wild curly hair cut into a trendy afro like the one she had, and made me up. Sparkling, I examined my reflection in the mirror. I looked like a fashionable young woman. Was it really me?

Luxuriating in Ms. Burke's vibe, I knew that I had found somebody who was on my side.

Chapter 37

I crouched down, then sat inside my suitcase, nestling amongst my glitzy stripper outfits. The memory of my pinched-off self who felt controlled by "the enemy", rocketed through me. "Never again," I growled.

I opened a notebook I'd brought in which I was revising the play about my family and smoothed its pages. *Once upon a time, there was a little girl and her family who were always hiding…*Finally I felt free to scratch down more truths. This was how I saw it and nobody was going to stop me from telling it, not anymore. Not Diddy, who had threatened to sue me if I wrote a play about our family. Not any anti-Semites. And most notably, I was no longer going to muzzle myself. I was even going to risk sharing what I learned working as a stripper.

I wrote about how as a teeny-bopper, I had graduated high school at the age of fifteen, by a whisker. Pining to be somebody different than myself, I immediately enrolled in a college Acting Program at the State University of New York.

Dad had supported my direction of study because I promised to come to Vienna to live with him after I graduated. Even though the thought of living with him made me feel puke-y, and in Vienna, Nazi central, I had ostensibly complied, "Great, Diddy!" I chirped, hoping that once I finished college, I could convince him otherwise. My acting skills were already serving me well.

Chapter 38

Diddy arranged for me to spend summer at the college dorm. I had seen Sean and Marcus a few times but had only spoken with my other siblings by phone very intermittently. And of course, under dad's ongoing scrutiny, visiting Momma was out of the question.

Being isolated on the largely deserted campus was a little "end-of-the-world-ish", but it was also calming. Dad phoned weekly, always ensuring that I hadn't leaked my Jewish identity or allowed any "dirty boys" near me, and we wrote each other every few days.

I became friends with a mixed-race gal named Daisy, who was a natural actress, and so stunning that she had graced the cover of *Eighteen* magazine. She remained cool under public examination, and I pined to attain her level of seemingly effortless comfort.

During Acting class, we were asked to write and perform an original monologue. Using real fruit as props, I impersonated my version of a bag lady. I attacked oranges with a shoe, speaking in a throaty voice, as they spattered. "I'll kill you, bastards!" I put the shoe on, and stepped on bananas, squashing them. "Traitors, Communists!" I grabbed a few strawberries and hurled them against the stage wall, splattering them. "How could you, how could you take her? A baby from her mother? Accuse a mother of poisoning her baby's food?" I paused, surprised by my raw connection to the material and the violence I expressed.

My teacher, Duke, an intense, middle-aged balding New York actor, jumped from his seat, exhorting me. "Good, don't stop. Show us your pain. Go!"

I picked up a bunch of grapes and rocked them like an infant. "Lucia, my baby, you're back. They brought you back, just to torture me. I'm sure they'll try to snatch you soon enough, but they'll never find you." I was fully connected, weeping. "We'll change our names, get our fingerprints altered, but I'll never leave your side. I'll always be your Momma. You won't ever be alone, even when I'm not here–" I sat in silence, sobbing, stroking my make-believe infant.

As the room applauded, I automatically smiled as big as the room. Duke stood as I broke out of character. "Good work, Frannie, but that's just the tip of the iceberg. You need to have the courage to reveal even more, dig deeper, no secrets here. Keep going. Improvise further with this character."

I picked up a peeled orange, squishing it in my hand. I continued, this time detached from my pain, unintentionally holding my breath. "One day, I will get them back for what they are doing."

Duke shouted mercilessly. "Stop! Again!"

My forehead itched, making me realize that I was sweating. "One day, I will get them back–" I reattempted.

Duke stood, turning to the class. "Who bought that, anybody?"

Nobody responded. He gave me a knowing look. This unpredictable emotional deadening while I was acting had happened several times in class before. It made me appear phony. *Did they suspect that I was really Jewish?* Something about my psychological circuitry was erroneous.

I moved around the stage, picking up the fruit residue. I had thought that using a character as a cover would allow me to hide, but it only worked once in a while.

"Every time, just when you get close to the meat of the truth, cop-out!" Duke's words stung like electric shocks, revealing me for the imposter I was. My mind was a nut house.

I slowly peered around the audience, frozen. I noticed my classmate, Lily, smiling compassionately.

I started towards the exit, muttering, "Need a-a break."

Duke called after me. "Uh-huh. Frannie, I know you're younger than anyone in the class, not including me." The class laughed. "But you have something special. You could be the best actress in the school.

You're a natural, but you just want to fly away like a little bird!"

I left the room, torn, sickened by my own limitation, as the class watched. Outside on the stone steps of the university's main building, the cold on my bum helped to numb me. I wrote in my journal for a while. Then I employed the tactic I had learned in boarding school. If I sat perfectly still for long enough and didn't make eye contact with anyone, it was as if I melded with the environment. I imagined morphing with the stone steps, pretending that I had become part of the building.

A few people from acting class walked by on their break and asked me what happened, but I didn't know what to say. "I need to be institutionalized, apparently," I quipped, which they found funny. Diddy often commented that there was a little truth in every joke. I longed to respond that there's a little joke in every truth!

But frustrating as acting classes were, when I did occasionally connect, it provided me with confidence to socialize and joke. Dad had told me that it was fine to get initial training in theater, but that it would not suffice as a sole degree. He said that during the next Holocaust I would need skills to be able to survive, and that there were three options; I could become a baker, a doctor, or a secretary. I asked whether I could become a milliner. I had loved playing dress up with mom's hat collection. But he said that a hat would not protect my head when bombs are falling out of the sky. I wanted to say, "Maybe so, but at least I would look striking while I was dying," but I knew better.

I secured a lead role in the play our freshman class presented and was touted as a "natural," and "way ahead of her much older peers." But still, I got caught in the same loop of emotional misalignment. I wasn't able to look people in the eyes any longer and they thought I was doing it intentionally.

"Why are you making my job such a nightmare?" the director shouted, aghast.

I fled rehearsal and locked myself in my dorm room. When I surfaced, I went to spend time with Lily, who I had developed a friendship with. But, considering my childhood indoctrination with stories about mental illness treatments, I didn't feel like I could disclose anything about my devastation at being emotionally blocked with her.

I was asked out on a date by an older boy. Wearing the flared white dress that I had worn to high-school graduation which I pulled off my shoulders, affixing a silk red flower in my hair -- I thought I looked pretty and slightly exotic. My fashion statement inspiration had been the actress Marlo Thomas, from the TV series *That Girl*, who had worn a similar ensemble during one episode. I was still a virgin and this was my first real date.

When Jorgen came to pick me up, I descended the dormitory stairs just as one of the most popular girls in the dorm dashed up. "You look like a hot whore. Wahoo!" she wisecracked.

My muscles seized up. I tried to soothe myself but couldn't. I continued down the stairs trying to breathe away the rock in my belly.

Jorgen was a cute, third year History major. I was hyper-vigilant that he might act lasciviously because of Diddy's incessant warnings, but he was a gentleman and was clearly awed that I was only fifteen.

He phoned the next day and telephoned for a couple of weeks but I ducked all of his calls. Although I found him attractive and had reveled in his attention, the possibility of a second date, leading to him getting to know what I believed was the real "broken" me, was out of the question.

One way I made myself feel better was to construct theatrical outfits. The local thrift store allowed students to fill a large plastic garbage bag with clothing for only a dollar. I put together what I thought was a classy, alluring forties look.

I walked towards the campus, sporting a skintight, navy blue pencil dress, stiletto boots, pillbox hat with netting, and gloves feeling like a movie star in somebody else's movie. A man sitting in a truck, rolled down his window and called, "Hey baby?"

"Yes?" I replied, trying to look as if I didn't expect a compliment.

"Halloween is over!" He chortled, then drove away.

I hustled back home and changed.

Lily had moved in with her boyfriend and was busy cocooning with him. As the weeks went by, I skipped school entirely, hiding in my room instead.

One day without warning, Diddy knocked on my bedroom door. Always a small man, now in his late sixties he was much shrunken, well under five feet. He refused to converse other than accusing me of being "completely crazy," and insisted that we leave for Canada the next day. Being under-age, I was trapped. I was never sure if he had enlisted someone to spy on me or not, or if the university administration had simply alerted him about my lack of attendance.

At the airport, he interrupted as I attempted to shift to positive talk about Lily. He leaned close, whispering, "I wouldn't be surprised if in the midst of your *farkakteh* – crazy behavior, you let slip to her all about your being Jewish!"

Grasping for levity, I covered my head with a scarf, and spoke with an over-the-top Jewish accent.

"Diddy, you don't need to be so vorried. I'm not stupid but I do have *ch-h-hutzpah* – shameless guts!"

He grabbed my arm, and pulled the scarf off my head, whispering hoarsely, "Keep quiet, foolish girl, you put us in grave danger! I have seen people killed for telling jokes! You never know who's listening!

You're untrustworthy, just like your mother!"

After a few strained moments, I blurted, "Lily's my friend, Diddy. She wouldn't ever–"

"My frie-e-end!" he mocked savagely. "You know nothing, you know less than nothing! You have no idea who your so-called friend is talking to right this very minute–" I tried to answer but he continued at me with machine gun like bursts, "right now, do you?"

I kept my eyes on him, crumbling under his relentless onslaught.

"Very immature behavior, Frannie, after everything I've done for you! You are getting older and must learn skills to make your way in the world. You need to attend classes like a normal person, cover your behind, complete university. To be truthful, I never thought this acting business was a good idea."

"Diddy, you might be right. I'm just not sure if I want to be an actress. I keep feeling like I want to do something that's more – me."

He laughed. "Me-shme! Nobody gives a hoot about feelings when people are starving to death! You need skills to survive. I tell you Frannie, the Holocaust is just around the corner. No artsy-fartsy nonsense, wasting your life. You learn something practical, then you come to live with me in Vienna."

My heart was rocking. "Well, I'll jump off that bridge when I get to it!"

"No jumping off bridges! You do what your dad says! You need some help, Frances! Keep your voice down; people will know you're not normal."

I struggled to find the right words, staring at the luggage. "Diddy, I'm not-not moving to Vienna. I'm going to try to write my own stuff."

He didn't say anything. I barreled ahead, finally looking up. "I want to go live with Momma!"

Dad glowered, nodding his head self-righteously. "You are making a big mistake, Frannie, living in a fantasy world! Cuckoo, just like your mother, who, by the way won't want you with her." He continued with a menacing smile, fishing bills from his wallet, and slamming them on the table. "Buy a ticket to her. After this, I no longer pay for you to waste my hard-earned money! How dare you go over to the other side, after all I've done for you! Let me know when you come to your senses. This is the last dollar you get from me!"

I hung my head. Dad adjusted his gloves. "I'm going to catch the next flight home." He pulled the heavy sleeves of his coat on over his small arms.

"Diddy, this is so silly – please don't leave!" Without looking at me, he wheeled his luggage away.

My stomach imploded. I got up and trailed him. "Diddy, I'm sorry!"

He kept walking, turning back once to call to me. "Too late for sorries."

Chapter 39

Dad's exiting line really chafed. Why did he make me feel like hell for wanting to be close to Momma? For wanting to reach for happiness and follow my own path? Is stripping getting me any closer to my truth? No matter how naked I get on stage I can't figure out what there is to feel bad about – the opposite is true.

A corner of my gold glitter tear-away skirt stuck out from my suitcase reminding me how comfortable I felt being physically bare and unguarded onstage and with people who weren't Jewish... except for the occasional film producer. And in my utter nakedness I felt connected to other human beings. I felt good about myself and safe in my bare skin.

I pulled out a photograph of dad which was sandwiched at the back of my journal. Looking at it made my mouth twist. It was one of the rare pictures of him for which he dressed casually, wearing a flannel shirt and suspenders. He was smiling sweetly and looked cuddly and cute. But I hadn't forgotten how his happy face could quickly transition into an ugly grimace.

"Momma wasn't the crazy one, Diddy, was she?" I mocked. "You said you were sending me away from home to protect me from my crazy mother. Hah! More like you were sending me away from your scary self, and from the "concentration camp" we kids called home!"

Comedy Club Palm Beach 2018

So, anybody celebrating anything tonight like a wedding anniversary, or a birthday, or surviving the Holocaust?

Hey, it's never too late to celebrate life -- any Vets here? You know what I'm talking about -- the motherfuckers can take everything from you, but they can't take your sense of humor! Humor literally keeps people alive --it gives you hope. So, when I heard comedian Sarah Silverman make the jokes: "You know who has a tiny vagina? Barbie. Not Klaus Barbie, the infamous Nazi. Nazis are a-holes, and I'll be the first one to say it -- because I'm edgy. Nazis are motherfucking asshole wipes. Dicks. Oh, they're cute when they're little, I will give them that. They're so cute: Why can't they stay small?" Sarah's Nazi humor made me roar with laughter.

Like, my parents are Holocaust survivors, so I've heard stories, and apparently some guy crammed in a cattle car on the way to concentration camp where everyone was frozen in silence --all of a sudden he goes, "Well, I guess first class...was full!" Listen, whatever gets you through the night, right? Humor, shrinks, group sex I mean therapy -- group therapy -- really. I went to group therapy with children of Holocaust survivors and someone shared that when she was a kid she loved her Barbie dolls but instead of playing y'know, 'Barbie Goes to the Hairdresser' or 'Barbie Goes To Malibu' she'd play 'Barbie tells the Gestapo about the Jews hiding in the attic next door and they go to Auschvitz'!

Chapter 40

When I first called to tell Momma that I wanted to visit, she had gone silent. I heard her blow her nose.

"'Scuse me. This is lovely, Frances. Are you coming in a few weeks or when were you thinking?"

"Tomorrow."

A few hours after I'd arrived at the Ottawa condo that she had purchased with alimony money from the divorce, we sat over tea and Mandelbrot at a small dining room table. That first day, we cried so much that by the time we got around to drinking, our tea had cooled.

"I went to the Hadassah Bazaar yesterday--like a flea market. Jewish." Momma said smoothing the tabletop. "We will go together sometime."

I smiled at her casual reference to include me in a Jewish event, as if doing so had been normal in our household.

She stroked my hand. "Beautiful long fingers."

She wordlessly got up and carried my bags into one of the empty bedrooms. I followed, noticing her blue-black hair was shot through with an abundance of steely greys.

"The bed is made up. I give you some time to settle in." She stared at me blankly. "I can't get over, my Frances! Is a young woman!"

I gazed out at the feather soft-looking cedar trees outside the bedroom window at my mother's home. I'd freed myself from capture. Bleary-eyed, I opted to crash instead of unpack.

When I woke, it was dark. It took me a moment to remember where I was. I opened the door and saw light coming from the room down the hall. Mother was entering what I realized was her room.

Except for panties, she was naked. Hearing my door open, she turned towards me. My mouth fell open. Her breasts hung almost to her waist.

"This is what it looks like after breast feeding seven children, Frances. You'll see!"

'Not me!' I thought, but I quickly said, "I love you, Momma."

It must've been a few hours later when she knocked on the door. "Coffee, sweetheart?"

"Sure."

Wearing her cozy, quilted, housecoat covered in red and orange flowers, she carried two cups into the dining room. It looked almost new, not because she hadn't worn it almost every morning, but due to her delicate touch which was always there when she felt good. "Just so happy you're here, Frances," she said, rubbing my cheek.

I smiled "Don't get me mushy again, Momma!"

"*Nein, genug* -- no, enough!" she said. "One minute. I have something I want to show you." She waltzed through the dining room towards her bedroom calling over her shoulder.

While she was gone, I noticed the sunken living room in front of me, furnished with velvet furniture and floor length gold drapes. She now had a place to feel proud of when company visited. Dad had refused to replace the badly worn carpet in our living room, or upgrade any shabby aspect of our childhood home.

Momma came back to the table, carrying a black book, on top of an album. She placed it down, and patted it, "I have photographs!"

I noticed that the book had a swastika on its cover. *Was this supposed to cheer me up?* I clenched upon seeing the sinister symbol. The book was *The Rise and Fall of The Third Reich,* the same book dad had in his study.

"I was thinking Frances, not that it's a light topic, but I never told you about what happened to your grandmother. I felt that I was doing the right thing. You were just a little girl."

"I know, mom. It's fine --Diddy told me that your mother was -- killed."

"I'm not surprised!" she said. "He did everything behind my back, the poor man!" she tsk-tsk'd her tongue.

I realized that as an adult, I was no longer irked by her idiosyncrasy.

"What a waste! We could have been so happy --" she sighed.

Perhaps the rush of emotion provoked by our reunion spurred mom to tell me, all at once, her history during the war. Really, I had no choice but to listen. She was unstoppable; we stayed up half the night and she told me what she remembered.

First, she shared that she had stuck it out with dad because the one thing she had yearned for more than anything was to have a happy Jewish home, like her childhood home had been in Bremen, Germany. She was born in 1921 to Selma and Josef Zwienicki and raised in a strictly kosher manner. The Zwienicki's owned a thriving bicycle and motorcycle sales and repair shop, essentially run by her mother who also offered beautiful handwriting skills, often free of charge, to customers who needed important letters written. Later on, this skill proved to be the Zwienicki's lifeline.

Momma said that even though anti-Semitism was ever present, being a social and popular girl, she attended school until Jews were banished. She told me how much she adored her little brother Alfred, and her big brothers Benno and Gerd. As the only girl in the family, she was particularly close to her mother. Her eyes danced as she told me about the Jewish rituals they shared.

But on November 9th, 1938, as the Zwienicki household slept, a loud rapping was heard at their door in the wee hours of the morning. They peeked out the window and saw brown shirts on the first-floor landing. Mom said that the tyrants had come because they knew that her dad, Josef was the *Shammas* --the synagogue caretaker, and had the responsibility to guard the keys to the synagogue.

My granddad managed to escape with the keys, over the rooftops, before the soldiers barged in.

Unable to locate what they wanted, they retaliated. They shot my grandmother, Selma, in front of two of her sons, Benno and Alfred, who saw her die. Alfred was beaten and soon after that night was caught and sent to *Sachsenhausen*. Gerd was not home -- he was being held in a Nazi prison cell at a police station in Wurzburg. Twelve-year-old Alfred was initially able to flee, and he hitchhiked, shoeless, the sixty miles from Bremen to Hamburg to see his seventeen-year-old sister, my mother. She was working as a nanny in Hamburg, being trained to run an orthodox Jewish household at the home of some wealthy people named the Hirsch's, who, she said, were very good to her. Alfred arrived on Shabbos, shoeless, to deliver the news of their mother's murder to her.

The Gestapo located Gerd and forced him to sign documents forging their mother's death. It stated that she had died of natural causes. "Monsters, real monsters!" mother said. Then she tapped the book on the table. "But the truth is in here, Frances. This 'William Shirer' book. *The Rise and Fall of The Third Reich*." She opened the book to page 582, and pointed to the footnote, reading out loud. "Major Buch's report gives an authentic picture of justice in the Third Reich." She looked at me. "Yes, they called killing Jews justice, Frances. It was legal to kill us for no reason at all. If you so much as sneezed and a Nazi disapproved, you were gone! I saw these things happen more than once. And worse, much, much worse! Ah, jah!" she exhaled deeply.

She continued, aloud. "Here Shirer cites --" she mumbled to herself, reading, moving her index finger ahead. "Here we are, Frances! The names of the murdered and the murderers. 'Party members Behring, Willi, and Heike, Josef, because of the shooting of the Jew Rosenbaum and --" She slid closer to me.

"You see here Frances? Where it says '--and the Jewess Zwienicki'?"

I nodded. "That was your grandmother, my lovely mother" she patted her chest, trying to compose herself, but welling up. She took both my hands in hers. "Never forget this Frances. Her murder took place on what's called Kristallnacht. The Night of Broken Glass."

"What broke Momma?" I asked, "Like windows and chandeliers? Or --"

Mom hurriedly stood and went into the kitchen. "What broke, Frances?" she called to me, forcing her voice. I realized that she was trying to calm herself. "My heart, Frances. That's what broke, my heart."

I went to her and put my arms around her. She told me that my grandmother had applied her handwriting skills by penning a heart-felt letter to my paternal cousins, who lived across the pond on a farm, appealing for sponsorship. Both an exit and an entrance visa were necessary. But at first the cousins had rejected them. "Nobody wanted us!" Momma said. "'None is too many!' is the famous phrase said by that bigot, Mackenzie-King! I wonder what he would have said if it had been his mother?"

I nodded. Mother said that after hearing about my grandmother's murder, they had conceded to help. Approximately a year later, after dodging many attempts by the Gestapo to thwart their journey, and a few miracles, a departure date was eventually set.

Mom nodded, remembering, smoothing the laminated book cover. "Jah. So, after Momma was gone, I remained in Bremen. To take care of Papa, Alfred, and Gerd. And before we left Germany, we paid a visit to Momma's grave, then boarded a train to Hamburg."

I wondered how my sweet-tempered Uncle Gerd had remained so courageously open about our heritage after having endured such horror. How had my uncle managed to live as Jew when my dad could not? Then it struck me that my mother had left someone out. "Didn't you have another broth --?"

"Benno. Jah. Frances, there is too much to tell at one sitting. Benno died in a car accident before we left. He was very shaken over my mother's death. So back to what I was saying --in Hamburg, we went to visit my aunt and cousins. Of course, they plead for help, Frances. But we had nothing to offer!" She shook her head. "All of them, victims of Nazi murder. Jah --" she looked away. "Life goes on, Frances.

So, jah, then–oh that ship! I vomited for weeks! We were just exhausted when we finally docked. But then a nun met us -- a volunteer. With a telegram. From the cousins. They had experienced financial hardships and suggested we didn't come to the farm. So, we didn't. But quite a bit later on, during happier times, I met your handsome dad!"

"That's right, Momma. Diddy mentioned that…where did you meet again?" I asked, grateful for the break from sadness.

She took my hand "Jah, important to have nice memories. So, one day while out for a walk --" she shook her head, smiling, "that is where Bernie and I first met. Oych, Bernie was so handsome." Her mouth fell open, as if she couldn't really believe it herself. "Here. I'll show you!"

Momma showed me a picture of them together. They glowed so much it made me say, "Oh-h-h!" They were huddled for the camera, open smiles, glistening eyes.

"Your dad was lovely to me, then." Her face clouded over. "Of course, how could I know what would come. He went through too much, we all did." She stood. "Soup?"

I nodded.

She continued to speak from the kitchen. "I'll warm it in the micro. Frances, did you know that we eloped?" she asked gleefully.

"Eloped? Wow. No." For the first time I imagined my parents, young and mischievous.

Momma continued. "Jah. Bernie and I were married in '46, in Buffalo. At Saranac orthodox synagogue. Jah, that was then." She reentered the dining room carrying a bowl of soup, the spoon already inserted in it. She placed the bowl in front of me. "Let the spoon cool it off for a minute. A trick from Good Housekeeping." She sat and flipped the page of the album, shaking her head. "Jah we were young and very much in love then. Yes, I'm talking about your dad. Mr. Pork Rinds!" she laughed to herself.

At the end of the album was a photograph of a gigantic stone structure which she stood next to, clustered with a group of women, their arms around each other. Mom explained that she had taken a trip back to Bremen for the unveiling of a shrine. It had been erected as a memorial to Kristallnacht, in memory of the victims who had lived in Bremen. "Jah, you see, Frances, this is the monument in Bremen, and my Mommas' name is etched on the stone."

"Who are all those women?"

She nodded, smiling. "Classmates. Jah. Greta here --" she looked up at me to make certain I saw which woman she was pointing to. The pretty, middle-aged woman was looking at my mother, smiling warmly. "Greta, was a Nazi, und-" She tossed out the words as if she had been telling me they had once worked as dental assistants. "Hindy, was a Nazi too und-"

"Momma!" I sputtered. "How, how could you stand to be in the same room as all those Nazis?"

She waved my thought away with her hand as if to suggest that I was being ridiculous. "Uch Frances, everyone was a Nazi! What you want me to do, hate them forever?" She pointed to the soup in front of me. "Take, eat, I made it fresh for you!" She smiled at me so sweetly I wished she would never stop.

I spent the night tossing and turning, and finally got up. Beethoven's 5th Symphony was coming from Momma's room. I knocked on her door.

"Jah? Come in, bitte."

She looked regal, holding her long white neck high, buffing her nails, perched on a padded, faux antique chair. When I was younger, she had shared that she believed she'd been royalty in a previous incarnation. Her old-world European elegance possessed a majesty which convinced me of the truth of her statement. Seeing her calm and ceremonious especially after all she'd withstood, was almost as good as one of her hugs.

"Have a seat, honey." she offered, glancing at me, mid-buff. "Having problems sleeping?"

Before I could answer she added, "It's to be expected, Frances. You've been through much too much!

And that's putting it mildly."

I flopped on her bed, bunching up a few decorative pillows under me. They had been flawlessly covered in silks and brocades, with tassels and ribbons. I knew they were her handiwork, being very similar in style to the fancy pillow slips she'd sewn, and covered the sofa throw pillows with in my childhood home. Contrasted against the threadbare living room couch, they had resembled fabric jewels.

I told mother that I was worried dad was feeling depressed about my having vanished from his life.

She shook her head slowly, and deliberately. "Uch, vus! Your dad can take care of himself. He has been very selfish and downright criminal, keeping you from me! If Bernie had it his way, we wouldn't be together now at all! It's a miracle that you found the strength to challenge him, and to come to me. I know how manipulative he is, Frances! Then he runs back to Vienna like a chicken with his head cut off!"

She examined my dour expression. "Frances, you can tell me; did Bernie ever abuse you? Touch you---?"

"Yuck! No Mom!" I replied, disgusted.

"It wouldn't have been a surprise if he had. Not that any of your sisters were violated by him. But you spent so many nights alone together."

I felt like I'd been dipped in something sticky and stinky. I got up and walked around her room, trying to make sense of her question. "Did you really think that was happening?

"I wasn't sure. He became a tormentor, your dad."

"But if you --why didn't you-?"

"Intervene?" she asked.

"I tried. If you remember."

I did recall that during one of his middle-of-the-night lectures, my dad had heard someone lurking outside his bedroom and opened the door to find my mother listening.

"And if you recall," said mom, "he repeatedly threatened to have me institutionalized."

"Well Momma, that night when you came to listen at the door, you could have brought the vacuum cleaner with you as a cover and told him that you were just about to start vacuuming the hall."

She looked at me quizzically.

"C'mon Mom, middle-of-the night cleaning would have made as much sense as his *farkakteh* -- crazy middle-of-the-night lectures!"

Momma shrugged "True. You don't think of these things at the time. I was very worried about you, Frances."

Warm honey ran through me hearing how concerned she'd been.

"These weren't empty threats from your dad Frances! Doctors have had their wives lobotomized, institutionalized, you name it! The irony! He is a sick man, your dad." She shrugged and sighed.

"That's life! Oy, at first we were so crazy for each other. So eager to make babies together, to make up for all our murdered loved ones."

It was startling to hear mother referring to the passion she'd shared with dad the dictator. It made me feel closer to her. But the direction of my parental allegiance had changed 180 degrees, and I frequently felt lost.

The next morning, I woke late, my body weighted down. I closed my eyes. Mother came in and gently shook me. It felt like an assault.

"Mother!" I shouted.

"It's a lovely, sunny day, Frances. We could go for a walk, have a nice celebration picnic in the--"

"Sh-h-h!" All I craved was more sleep. I lied and told her that I had a bug. She took my temperature and brought me water, soup, and dry toast. It was my seventeenth birthday. I slept all day and kept up the same behavior for almost two weeks.

When I drifted up from sleep, I found mom opening the curtains. She said that she wanted to bake me a birthday cake. Over-sensitized, I could barely tolerate the daylight coming through the windows, let alone think about blowing out candles.

Momma told me that we would get through it together. I stayed there all day. Sometimes, she came in and stroked my head, and told me about my siblings, who was doing what and where. Although I had been closest to Sally due to dad having made us his favorites, I had long ago adapted to being without her. I wasn't surprised to hear that Marcus had been having problems coping with life, considering the numerous times dad had called him "crazy". She told me that Marcus was on a road trip with a friend and was coming back to live with her.

I decided to get a job. Having grown my nails "Barbara Streisand-length", paired with my curly black afro, it allowed me to appear a little older. Even though I was underage by a year, I secured a waitressing job in an all-night licensed diner and became fast friends with another waiter; friendly, funny Kenny, an up-and-coming ballet dancer. After work, he would take me out to nightclubs where he flirted with other gorgeous gay men. I loved the music and the live-and-let live atmosphere; I danced my fanny off.

One day, a few months after returning to mom, I realized that I was smiling for no reason. And then, the phone rang. Momma quickly handed me the receiver. "It's your dad!" It turned out that he hadn't gone to Vienna after all. He was in town and had rented an apartment downtown. He spoke to me in his "happy dad" voice, which made me bubble. I agreed to visit.

Chapter 41

I dawdled towards his apartment, pop rocks dancing in my middle. The door opened before I got to it. He was wearing his red flannel shirt, which gave him a deceptively relaxed look. I smelled sausages and could hear the sound of oil frying.

"Hello Sweetheart, come in come in!" Diddy hugged me tightly, gazing with great affection. Although I was attempting to remain on alert, I heard myself sigh.

"Are you hungry? I'm cooking bratwurst. Come we have some nice lunch together."

I chewed the delicious fatty meat dipped in sweet brown mustard, while dad outlined his new plan for me. "Und after you register at secretarial college, I will return to Vienna and resume studying at my old alma mater. I plan to do a second PhD. Then, when you graduate, you come to me and I will have a job waiting for you; either with United Nations or another prominent institution. You need secretarial skills to be able to be useful during another Holocaust --things look very bad, Frances. There is another Holocaust brewing right around the corner! And the Reinhardt Seminar --you remember the famous theater institute, Frances? It's right there."

As much as I knew that I was falling back into the wormhole, the familiarity of Diddy weaving a web of protection pacified me. It was as if he held the magic wand to properly direct the movie of my life and however much I might not enjoy my role, I trusted that the script he created would not have my character end up in a mental institution.

I quit my waitressing job and registered for a secretarial program at Algonquin College. After the first mind-numbingly boring week, I found myself sitting in front of a typewriter, fingers frozen on the keys. I got up and walked the halls, feeling incarcerated.

An exquisite, fine-boned woman approached me. "Hi, I'm Jan," she extended her hand and didn't let go. "I'm in your typing class. How are you?"

Perhaps it was partly because she was a stranger, but the sincerity of her concern caused me to come undone. After sharing my story, she assured me that secretarial school was not my only option but suggested that I check with the school psychologist for a professional evaluation.

Dr Martin smiled widely, then pointed to a comfy leather chair across from her desk. I sat and she leaned forward to hear what I had to say.

"I want to leave school -- it just doesn't feel like me."

"You sound pretty certain. So, what's stopping you?"

"Well, my dad told me that if I don't have secretarial skills, I won't survive another Holocaust."

She burst out laughing and had a hard time containing herself, even though I was visibly squirming.

"Really? That's absurd. You can find lots of ways to survive. Holocaust?"

I felt the heat on my cheeks and knew that my face had turned an undeniable shade of shame-red. *She thinks I'm crazy. Maybe Diddy was right. She's a professional, so I am. Only a crazy person would have believed his lies.* But how could dad have lied to me? Over and over about an impending Holocaust? I felt like such an idiot for having believed him. Stomach acid shot up into my esophagus making me cough. The doctor handed me a bottle of water. I nodded thanks and gulped. I couldn't digest how dad had the audacity to drill into me that if I didn't follow his orders I wouldn't survive. Survive? He was killing me. Hah! Move to Vienna? Not fucking likely! And what kind of Monster would wedge himself in between me and Momma?

And just like that, Dr. Martin's unaffected reaction burst down my wall of confusion. Thanks to Momma having verified that dad was emotionally unstable, the doc's opinion lifted any residual murkiness that his Holocaust-anoia was cuckoo. Here was an adult authority -- a doctor! -- telling me that what Diddy had led me to believe about the world was simply untrue, such as that everyone was out to get me because I was Jewish, and that big-mouthed Jews were institutionalized, that dirty boys were out to touch me, that the reason I was sent to boarding school at the age of eleven was to be kept away from mom because she was unstable and I was becoming crazy like her, and that listening to my gut when I defended her meant that I was supporting her unstable behavior making me crazy by proxy.

Although I experienced relief now knowing the truth, I also felt like a buffoon for having been deluded.

After leaving the secretarial program I continued to live at mom's. I allowed myself to begin again to dream of becoming an actress. I auditioned for a role in the Ottawa Little Theater's production of A.R. Gurney's "Children," and secured the lead role of Barbara. Rehearsals were a combination of fun and frustration as my old succubus always managed to rear its head just when my performance was the most natural and raw.

Both Kenny from the diner and Jan from secretarial college attended dress rehearsal, during which I managed to let go. They assured me that it was evident from my performance that I knew what it felt like to be someone else. It bolstered my confidence to move to a bigger city, where I'd have the opportunity to pursue a professional acting career. Maybe Toronto. It was just a few hours away.

But in the meantime, since Momma and I were still living under the same roof, although I was skeptical whether she would enjoy it, I invited her to see me perform the role of Barbara in the Gurney play. She didn't come. I didn't noodle her about it because the show spoke to family unhappiness and she'd experienced enough for twenty lifetimes.

One day after the run had ended, while fluffing the cushions of her velvet sectional, she suddenly spat, "Do you really hate me as much as Barbara talked about?"

"What? Do you mean my character in the play, Momma? Mom, it's a play. How do you know that about my character? Did you read the script or something?"

"Well, I saw it three times and you were very believable!"

My breathing quickened. I blanched, concerned that the new-found intimacy I'd discovered with mother was ephemeral. "It's a play Momma. My character and also the actor who plays my brother are upset at our family in the play. In the play, Mom. There are always some parallels in real life to what is written in plays, Mother! Please don't take it out of context. I mean think about how different it is to our story -- the actors who play the children are furious because their house is going to be sold. Obviously, that's not our real-life situation, Mom. Okay, in the play the children's unhappiness causes their mother to confront where her life with her husband has brought her...I get why that resonates with you personally. But otherwise, it's obviously a theatrical story which has nothing to do with us. I wish you would have told me. The only reason I didn't push you to come in the first place is because I was worried that this was going to happen!"

"Okay, okay," she sadly sang, running her fingers along a vase to check for dust.

I hugged her, "Momma, the vitriol Barbara spat...not about you!"

"Jah, Frances. Momma understands. I'm just upset in general!" She slumped onto the sofa, weeping. "I miss your dad--"

"You miss Diddy?"

"I know, it's crazy. I should never have left him."

Momma's grief seemed bottomless, and her crying became a daily ritual. I tried to employ some of the acting techniques I'd learned in university to help her move past the pain. Sitting at the dining room table with her when she was really overcome, I'd instruct, "Pound the table, Momma! Transform your pain to rage --get angry at him! Let it out!" Each time she'd accept my direction, pound the table and then burst out laughing, which was contagious.

But other than fleeting happiness, Momma's depression deepened. I now know that the unthinkable atrocities and losses she'd suffered in her youth, and then with my dad, had eaten away at her resilience. There are some tortuous emotional states which require a type of emotional realignment which I didn't know how to offer.

Marcus arrived and at first his good humor made us glisten. But on a dime, he'd become extremely moody saying things like; "I'm a bad person, Frances. I've done things and people know! The people I ran into in the hallway wouldn't even look at me!"

Although I was only slowly learning how to navigate my own emotions, I was able to suggest that he not give a shit about what people were thinking. But he wouldn't listen. He'd often shout, "I need to be alone!" then march into mother's extra bedroom and slam the door.

Looking out the window in my room, I noticed that the cedar tree had become tinged brown from windburn. I decided to relocate to Toronto but hadn't saved much money. Sensing my restlessness, Marcus generously offered me nine hundred dollars he had saved from odd jobs. This from a guy who believed he was bad.

Momma took me to the bus station, where we behaved like statisticians who were doing a test run of a trip. But as I waved to her through the window, I noticed her reddening nose and puffy eyes which caused me to whimper. Had we not stuffed down our tears before I boarded, I would never have left.

Chapter 42

After unpacking in the tiny apartment which I'd secured, I walked around to take in the downtown bustle of the bright big city. But after a few hours, my adrenalin dwindled, and the neon lights on the shops made my head pound.

I called mother who sweetly said, "Stick it out a little longer. Things will turn around, my peach."

But, for the next few days, I only hid in my new home, surviving on sandwiches she had packed.

Now that I was eighteen and able to legally work in a bar, I began cocktail waitressing at an upscale jazz club. I got off on the upbeat groove. Although it was the eighties, and disco was huge, there was something about jazz, and jazz fusion in particular which soothed me. Still, the slightest negative comment from another waitress or snarly customer stung.

A tall, handsome trumpet player would bow as I walked by, and coo, "Hello Pretty Lady." I was flattered when he asked me to accompany him to an after-work party.

It was a slow night, so we left shortly after 10 p.m. En route, he told me that he needed to make a quick stop, to give his wife a check. Before I could say, "You're married?" he got out of his snazzy red Corvette. It was dark out and I didn't know where we were. Ten minutes later he returned, slammed the door, and shouted, "fucking bitch!" He then pounded the steering wheel. The insult felt directed at me. I couldn't speak and moved to get out but he started to drive. Maybe I misjudged him. He was probably abused and justifiably angry. Besides, he'll know that I'm crazy if I get out. Eventually he calmed down somewhat. I likely miscalculated the situation. Was his wife truly the enemy?

He drove us to an affluent section of the city, to a darkly lit brick mansion where he became the jovial person he had originally appeared to be. But then, he flippantly introduced me to the owner who he referenced as a music producer. Having ridden out many of Diddy's outbursts, I told myself that the majority of the musicians' dark mood had dissipated. I was curious about what else the evening might bring.

A few people were sitting in a front lounge area engrossed in a meeting. We were quickly ushered past them to a bar area, deeper in the vast, antique-laden home. The musician and his friend whispered to each other while pouring us rum and cokes behind the counter. What was their secret? My gut clamped, but I tried to ignore it although I guessed that they were being covert because they thought that there was something wrong with me. Dad had driven that message home to me in numerous ways over the years and it was stuck inside.

Stuffing my feelings, I sat at the bar and sipped the drink they served. Then abruptly, I felt very drunk. I tried to focus, but everything was hazy. Was I sleeping? I was being led somewhere, behind some doors. It was dark. I couldn't speak. Extremely sleepy. He pulled my pants down. No. This is wrong. Stop. Can't move. He's inside me. Ramming my hips too hard. Stop this. Can't speak. This is wrong. Stop. Sleepy. Are we going to sleep?

When I woke I didn't know where I was. My clothes were half off. It was pitch black. Where the hell am I? Feeling around I seemed to be on a bed. I found the floor and half-crawled, half-walked, trying to find a wall. My vagina was sore. Did we have sex? I couldn't remember having fooled around earlier at all. Had I hurt myself?

I walked and walked then saw a slit of light --a door. I opened it. The musician and his friend were still at the bar. They turned and saw me. I smiled but they acted like they hadn't seen me, and turned away.

"What happened?" I asked, groggy.

"You passed out. Pig!"

What? How could he talk to me that way? Why didn't I have the strength to respond? I was too woozy to feel shame. I couldn't remember drinking more than a few sips. "Where's the bathroom?"

"We need to go." The trumpet player gruffly moved me out the door saying, "She had too much to drink. You're embarrassing!"

I tried to engage in conversation to find out the details. Tight-lipped, he drove me home. The sun was just starting to rise. I checked my watch. It was 5 a.m.

"Get out!" I did, and he banged the car door shut.

The next day my groin was bruised.

Back at work, I attempted to speak to the musician, but he darted away as if I was contaminated. It hurt, even though somewhere deep down I believed that I was tainted. Diddy's programming had long-lasting effects. But what horrible thing had I done at the mansion? I couldn't remember a thing. I stayed awake many nights trying to jog my memory. Months later, when I first began to remember the rape, slowly, in tiny flashes, I thought I was recalling a bad dream. But as the pieces became clearer, my feeling of degradation deepened. And I didn't tell anyone. Not even Momma. But I soon stopped working at the jazz joint, and I promised myself not to trust men.

As a young woman I hadn't realized that my father's consistent assessment that my opinions were those only a crazy person would make would destroy my ability to trust my survival instincts. Every time I had stood up to him when he put my mother down, or stood up for myself when I countered his endless need to share his painful stories, he accused me of being clinically emotionally ill and often threatened to have me institutionalized. At the time the path of least resistance was to continue to be a container for his pain. Since I didn't have any physical scars to prove that abuse had occurred, somewhere I blamed myself. So as an adult, why would I suddenly trust my gut when I was in the company of someone else who acted emotionally abusive?

---

https://mannettemorgan.com/blog1/domesticviolencepart2

Chapter 43

Standing in the scalding, chlorine-scented shower in my room above the strip club, partially anaesthetized by muscle relaxants, I mentally surveyed the rocky road I'd been on since my big city rape.

I joined a film acting class. A handsome young man with thick, choppy shoulder length brown hair named Keanu, began chatting with me. Whenever he walked into the room, it seemed as if he was surrounded by some kind of electrical current. He had previously shared with the group, that he'd been cast in a few films, and would be costarring in an upcoming movie that was still in development called, *Bill & Teds Excellent Adventure*.

"Frannie, I think we hang out at some of the same places," he said, smiling warmly.

Hot acid ran through my veins. I could barely speak. And it wasn't due to how attractive he was. He was a few years younger, and I had deemed him wrong for a romantic interest. I shook my head no.

"Ye-e-es!" he repeatedly nodded, being playful.

"No!" I hung my head.

"We should hang out!" he persisted.

I shook my head and walked away, finding a seat in the back.

The following week on my way to class, he noticed me while he was locking his motorcycle.

"Hey Fran! Good to see ya!" he said removing his motorcycle helmet and tossing his hair into place. "I'll walk in with ya -- did you memorize your scene?"

"Nice to see you Keanu. Yup!" I replied. Memorizing wasn't my stumbling block. I was dreading my old demon surfacing again,

163

which still happened almost every other time I got up in front of the class to perform. Still, the taste of freedom I sporadically felt while acting had planted an enormous hunger in me. I had to master it. It felt like flying.

A few days later, I bumped into him at a grocery store. He was flanked by two attractive young women. One was gently massaging his bicep, like she was tenderizing it.

"Hey Fran, how's it going?" he asked, freeing himself to adjust one of the dozens of safety pins in a pair of avant-garde jeans he was wearing. I had never seen such a funky pair of denims.

"Um, y'know, I'm doing well. Cool jeans."

One of Keanu's female guardians moved in front of him, "Keanu is doing re-e-eally well!" she announced, eyes widening.

He walked away from her. "Stop. Glad to hear everything's cool, Fran."

She leapfrogged in front of him again. "He is doing re-e-e-ally, really well!"

"Cut it out!" he giggled, moving away.

I was certain that they were high on ecstasy or some mind-altering equivalent.

"Anyway Fran, sincerely happy you're doing well, and --"

The other gal interrupted, "Yeah, but Keanu is doing really, really, really well!"

As the girls cackled together, I stepped in and kissed him full on the lips. When I came close to him, I felt some kind of energy. I couldn't put my finger on it but it was almost as if he was buzzing.

"Now, he's doing really, really, really, really well!" I laughed heartily. I blew him a kiss while I trotted towards the exit. "Have a great day, Keanu."

"I am now," he added, as I left the store without buying anything.

I'm certain he's never gotten over it, ha-ha.

Looking back, I have to say that I've never known anyone with the star power of Keanu Reeves who was completely a normal, considerate person. It's one of my fondest memories. In a world of show business where everyone presumes they are special and above the crowd, Keanu, who had a star aura around him -- unlike anyone I've ever met -- seemed oblivious to his own uniqueness.

Back in acting class, although he tried to playfully engage, I acted aloof -- and as if nothing had happened. I was far too distracted by my own challenges. Confused, I decided that perhaps I wasn't cut out to be an actress and threw myself into studying jazz-ballet. But then came the day in the dance studio when I found myself staring at a crack in the mirror and I felt split in two. Bam! The tug of war between the part of me that moved freely, and the part of me that cared more about what people thought of me -had taken center stage. So, I turned my energy to sketch comedy and auditioned for a class at Second City. A master teacher told me he thought I was gifted. He suggested that I audition for their touring company immediately, something he said was never done.

At the audition, impersonating a character, I played freely off another improviser, but then, as always, after a certain amount of open sharing, bam!

Stuck, I became engulfed in a prison of "disesteem". Many sleepless nights later, an inner voice whispered, *tell your story, tell your story*. Having fallen in love with stand-up comedy through watching comedians on television from the first day my father bought me a TV for my eleventh birthday -- Lucille Ball, Joan Rivers and Whoopie Goldberg just to name a few of my favs, I decided to try writing about life in a stand-up comedy format. The idea of striking back at things that bothered me, with humor, appealed. I was very inspired watching Billy Crystal when he impersonated his flatulent grandpa. Maybe I could find something funny about Diddy? Perhaps the blocks I suffered were a result of not having yet expressed myself through an artistic medium which was a better fit? Perhaps standup would allow me to be freer in public.

After the Emcee introduced me, I came onstage during open-mic night at the most well-known comedy club in Toronto, called Yuk-Yuks. I was petrified to just be myself. Instead, I hid behind a character by impersonating an elderly street person. Having been raised to believe that the world was cruel and out to get me, I felt great empathy for victims.

Sitting onstage, I stole an idea from one of Howie Mandel's performances during which he ordered from an invisible waiter. My character also spoke to a make-believe waiter while I requested a glass of champagne, then opened a gigantic purse (which I'd purchased at a thrift store), pulled out a real raw chicken and began to eat it. The audience screeched. It was hell trying to bite through the cold, rubbery flesh. Still, the crowd's engagement caused a rush of energy to surge through me. Focusing my adrenaline shot terror I attacked the bird with a vengeance. Having been raised by a mother who enforced stringent rules to do with food, I was fascinated by sloppy eaters and people who were downright abusive with it. It seemed freeing.

In retrospect, how I didn't die from salmonella poisoning is anybody's guess!

But at the time, all I cared about was how delightful it felt hearing the scrumptious sound of laughter in reaction to my comedic choices. It was delicious to exhibit outrageous behavior to do with eating, since food had been fascistically regulated at home. I enjoyed imbuing a vagrant with such a shocking trait, immediately transforming her from a helpless victim to someone who held comedic power.

I began performing at amateur nights without the façade of a costume, wig, and accent. But my old *mishegas* --craziness returned. I heard the other comics discuss stage fright, but from their description I knew I was dealing with something more complicated. They could generally find a way to control their fear. But every time I performed, I'd ultimately find myself pacing the stage shaky, dry-mouthed, often unable to recall any of the words I'd memorized, and unable to breathe. Still, like emotional crack, I ached for another fix of luscious laughter, even for a few minutes.

One night onstage, forcing myself to stand still, I willed myself to breathe. Looking out at the darkness under the blinding glare of the spotlight, I couldn't see a thing. I was carrying a fork and knife as props to aid with an impression I'd practiced. A male voice from the audience slurred, "Hey, wazza knife fer?"

Shot with adrenalin, I willed myself to focus and think about a sentence which I had repeatedly rehearsed *I am sane, I am funny, I am sane, I am funny…*

Just as I began to experience calm, he continued, "Hey girlie, anybody home? I asked ya what the fuckin' knife's fer'?"

I sweetly responded, "What's it for?" Then instantly, I shifted to a mock-evil tone. "To cut off your left testicle!"

The audience roared at the unexpected twist. "That's what it's *fer*" I continued, mocking his pronunciation, which extended the laughter. "And the forks because I'd rather not touch it!"

I had them, but I didn't know what to do with them. I was entirely unfamiliar with feeling this powerful, especially in public. I stayed there speechless for a few seconds, but the better part of me had already left. Then I quickly uttered, "Goodnight!" and left.

The Emcee said, "Hey, that was brave! Let's give her a nice round of applause for effort!" My gut rocked as the audience applauded, I knew somewhat obligatorily. But I was high from the few moments which I had successfully commanded the crowd.

As I walked alone backstage my act began to come back. Then a forty-ish year old man walked by. I overheard some of the other open mic'ers and comedians talking about him. Mark Breslin, who owned the YukYuks clubs, and also worked as a comic himself.

Then unexpectedly, he approached me, smiling warmly. My heart raced, but his chocolate brown eyes danced as he introduced himself, soothing me a little. He told me that I had great improvisational instincts and courage. That I was way ahead of most comics in that way, especially those my age. He said he was going to connect me with the club coach, Larry Horowitz and it wouldn't cost me anything.

I began to learn joke-writing from Larry, who was very affable. Yet despite their encouragement, almost always, moments after I'd walk onstage, I'd lose it. I adopted an iron-clad focus on the recitation of my jokes. But in doing so my shtick came off affected--the very antithesis of stand-up comedy.

In my apartment, I began to ingest entire containers of peanut butter and honey. I'd sit in a chair for expanses of twenty-four hours, trying not to move, or breathe, or feel.

But even after numbing myself with food, I continued to hunger for the exquisite freedom I'd felt those intermittent times when I'd been almost oblivious to what others thought of me onstage -- the complete opposite behavior to what had been repeatedly engrained in me. I was determined to win against my invisible enemy. The idea of making fun of forbidden things turned me on.

On the following open mic night, I took the microphone with practiced buoyancy. "Happy to be here even though I'm exhausted

--worst nights' sleep. Doesn't it suck when those middle of the night thoughts wake you up? - Y'know 'You need to make more money!' or whatever? Last night they were at me nonstop. 'You are the sexiest gal and everyone wants you! – I was like 'shutup, shutup, shutup! I was awake for hours…masturbating!"

The audience roared, zinging me with adrenalin. I fluffed my hair in the same way that Mae West had in a video I'd watched. Charged, I forged ahead.

"So how you guys doing?"

A man yelped, "Great!"

"That's just great!" I mocked, subtly attacking. Even though his vibe had been positive, having been deeply conditioned to expect that a negative attack was impending, I was on the alert for a nasty barb, or an anti-Semites' bullet. You never knew, Diddy had repeatedly warned. But I managed to continue on the comedic warpath. "Nobody is, you know, depressed, or horny?"

The audience giggled, filling my needy void with warm goo. I followed my instinct to further engage the receptive crowd, to set up my next joke. I spotted a couple. "How long have you two been together?"

They responded in unison. "Twenty-one years."

"Everything great?"

They nodded.

"Great, that's just great, great! Things still spicy?"

Their silence spoke for them, drawing audience laughter.

"Thought so! Well good for you for sticking with it anyway. Now, I don't mean to sound unromantic, but I imagine things can get boring after that amount of time, so why not at least be practical? Multitask!

Do it doggy-style 'cuz then at the same time you can get all your laundry folded."

The crowd howled at the joke I'd rehearsed, flooding me with glee and encouraging me to finish it.

I continued the bit "…you know eat some chips, file your nails, play a little bingo." I began to mock moan, "Oh baby, oh baby, oh-h-h." I looked at a make-believe bingo card. "O-64! Bingo!'

The audience cackled. I ended my set triumphantly, yet still fighting intermittent flashes of shame from having sex talked.

Mark bounced up to me. He said it was my best joke thus far. He suggested I employ "air humping"

while delivering the doggy-style lines to really drive it home. Flattered, I took the note.

Although I had been victorious, the following week onstage, I couldn't feel, couldn't think. I stood still, locked in terrifying silence, waiting to be called out for the imposter that deep inside I believed I was.

Somebody in the audience yelled, "Goodnight!"

I muffled a barely audible "Goodnight" and ran offstage. I hid in the shadows backstage, dreading contact. They know I'm crazy.

I heard Marks playful voice. "Fah-h-h-ra-a-anie, can I speak with you?" I prepared to weather the scolding I felt was imminent, considering how badly I'd failed.

But once I turned and looked at Mark who was about my height, I saw the sincerity and warmth in his eyes. "Frannie, your comedic instincts are brilliant when you get out of your head. You just need what I call "shock treatment."

That's it, he knows I'm crazy. But, I forged ahead, quipping. "Have you been talking to my parents?"

He laughed, not realizing the truth I'd revealed.

"Look, your energy and originality remind me of some very successful comics. We discovered Howie Mandel. Jim Carrey started here. I want to throw you in front of a large audience at a convention on Sunday. It'll terrify you, and either drive you to completely follow your instincts, or lose it. All you gotta do is five minutes, I'll give you a hundred if you do the gig -- if you do well, there will be more."

My euphoria only lasted for a moment. "Sunday?" *I-I'll bomb, again. He'll hate me. I can't.* "Maybe in a little while down the road," I said. "See, it's been too up and down, and I-I panic and I don't know why, I don't know. I'm sorry."

"Hmmm" He waddled his hips back and forth, mulling, then pointed at me. "You're Jewish, right?"

I held my breath.

"Right?" he repeated.

I nodded, trying to look like I thought it was a very normal question, but my gut was a fist. Is he really a good guy or an evil elf, like Diddy? Be careful.

169

He continued, "Your parents Holocaust survivors by any chance?"

I gulped and nodded.

"Thought so! Well, most comics are Jewish, and most comics should be in therapy!" He waited for the laugh that should have been there if he hadn't been talking to a walking open wound. "I've been going my whole life. Why don't you see somebody?"

I rubbed my right thumb against my index and third fingers, miming money.

"The Holocaust Center has a bargain for Jews, called 'group therapy'."

I smiled. "I don't know --maybe I'm just not cut out to be a comic."

He angled his eyebrow as if to say who you trying to kid?

"Okay, okay. I'll check it out, I will. Thanks."

He really sees me, I thought.

Little did I know that I had met a guy who built an empire for Jewish comics, who would help me immeasurably because he'd met similar people.

Chapter 44

I opened the door halfway to the Holocaust Center, the only Jewish building I had ever knowingly entered. My underarms felt sticky. I wished I hadn't worn my favorite pink angora sweater. I wondered if there were security guards in the vicinity, should an anti-Semite create a problem.

"Are you going in, or can I squeeze by?" asked a pretty, curly-haired woman.

My chest clenched. Had I offended her? Diddy had said that when someone willingly converts to Catholicism, Jewish people consider it the worst betrayal.

"Oh, I-I didn't realize anyone was behind me. Sorry, I'm going in."

"No problem," she said smiling pleasantly.

I walked in, a tad emboldened by her warmth. Spying an ornamental Star-of-David statue brought tears to my eyes. Momma had shown me a tiny fourteen carat gold Star-of-David pendant on a chain which she bought at the Hadassah Bazaar. I quickly dabbed the moisture from my eyes. I felt like an alien. A freak. I didn't want anyone to think that I was crazy.

I located the bathroom and hid in a stall. After a few minutes, I managed to convince myself that being late for the meeting would be worse.

Twenty minutes later, I found myself shuddering mid-group therapy, sitting together with participants ranging in age from twenty to ninety.

The gathering was led by the woman who I had blocked at the front door --a therapist named Marilee who oozed genuine sweetness, a welcome anchor in the room drenched in pain. I met a young woman around my age, a child of Ludolf von Fritsch (*Ludolf von Fritsch's name is an alias*), a decorated SS Officer, brimming with shame that didn't belong to her, but to her dad. She was unable to make eye contact with any of us Jews.

"I have his eyes, I have my dad's eyes," she wept.

I felt like she was talking about me. I gushed tears. Marilee asked me to tell the group about myself. I stalled with; "I'm Frannie and I'm not an alcoholic! But – to be truthful, I do have a little bit of an addiction – a codependent love affair going on with *Lindt* milk chocolate bars, but anyway…" a few people giggled. I took a breath. "Okay, well…my parents were Holocaust survivors, mom from Bremen, dad from Vienna. Many of their family members were murdered, they went through assaults, tortures you name it and got out by a whisker before being shipped off to the camps and --"

"Then they weren't Holocaust survivors. They were survivors of the Holocaust!" shouted one of the older men who looked like elder Kirk Douglas. "You don't get to call yourself a Holocaust survivor without one of these!" He pointed to the numbers on his arm.

I felt like I'd been slapped. How dare he denigrate my parents! "I'm sorry, I didn't realize there was a distinction," I quipped, heart racing, hoping he might soften.

"Well, there certainly is. And it's a big one. Seems like everyone wants to be a Holocaust survivor when they aren't eligible," he replied, playing the room.

I thought about leaving, but decided to stay after noticing that only a few of the older people were nodding in agreement.

Maybe because I had been programmed daily to protect my father, but an uncontrollable surge of heat caused my face to redden. I couldn't go without defending him.

Heart racing, I jibed, "Whoa, I didn't realize there was a pecking order! Do the lower numbers get better seats here?"

He answered with so much wrath, it was as if he was nailing me to a cross with each word. "This isn't a subject for laughter, young lady!"

My head was pounding. Was I going to be attacked? Should I run? I was glad I said what I did. I could literally hear the blood beating in my ears. Should I tell him how Diddy was nearly killed by an anti-Semite in 1951?

Everyone in the room was staring. I could hardly think. Then, I remembered to take a breath. "Forgive me, Sir, but I don't think it's a subject for false pride either. I mean, really -- is this some kind of weird competition? Like what about the other people who survived genocide like you know the Cambodians, or Africans or...? Isn't there enough misery to spread around without turning on one another for something this petty?"

The elderly man stood, extending his thumb and forefinger to make his hand resemble a gun. He pointed it at me, then continued hoarsely, "What would you know about suffering?"

I looked away to get my bearings, as people mumbled to each other. I thought about my uncle Alfred who the Nazis sent to *Sachsenhausen* when he was just a boy, after my grandmother Selma Zwienicki had been murdered on the night of broken glass. How preposterous it would be if he and my mother were asked whether they were Holocaust survivors, but only he was allowed to say, "I am!"

I turned to my accuser, who had sat back down, and was chatting with the "choir".

"Sir, I needed to gather my thoughts for a minute before answering your question, as to what I would know about suffering, and --"

"And?" he scoffed.

"And, no rivalry from me. But, I will share that both of my grandmothers and my grandfather were murdered by the Nazis including oodles of relatives not to mention the rapes and assaults foisted upon those who survived in the woods, fighting back and hiding. My father was nearly murdered several times and then nearly killed by Nazis in North America and so traumatized he made us hide our Jewishness and raised us Catholic. He sent me off to boarding school when I was eleven, drove away my mother and made most of us half-crazy, the rest, totally crazy, uh...Listen Sir, the war may have ended in Europe but its far-reaching fingers raged on within those of us of the next generation, within me. So, if I tell you more will I get a better seat? My *tuchas* --bottom is a little sore from the lack of padding on this chair!"

A few people laughed, including the therapist. He stared through me. An elderly woman got up and walked towards me, feet splayed like a ballerina. Her arms were surprisingly well-defined for someone of her advanced age. She squeezed and patted my arm. "I like you, Frannie. It's about time somebody told that old whiner to get a life. You seem pretty together. What are you doing here?"

"Thank you," I smiled. "What's your name?"

"Selma Rosenblatt" Chills went through me.

"Wow, Selma. Same name as my grandmother."

She nodded. "I was lucky. Escaped right after Kristallnacht, my husband not so lucky. Had to make a whole new family. I am a Holocaust survivor no matter what Mr. Fuckface over there says!"

A guttural laugh emerged from somewhere so deep inside of me, it was as if it had been stuck there for decades. I got up and hugged her.

Marilee approached. "I think you'll fit in here just fine, Frannie." She turned to the room, "Heads up Everyone! Okay group, you've listened to Frannie's opinion. What are your thoughts?"

My opposer barked, "She needs to respect the difference between Holocaust survivors and survivors of the Holocaust."

A few people groaned.

Then Selma interjected, "Morris, I think it's time you let that go. You're a good-looking man. You should get on with life while you're still young enough to enjoy. Why don't you come to one of my ballroom dance classes?"

"You think I'm good looking?" he replied almost smiling.

One of his cronies sitting next to him chimed, "You think he's still young?"

I laughed, grateful for the diversion.

"Frannie, I'm Sidney Hoffman," an old man yelled from the back of the room. "You are very welcome here, and many of us agree with you. Now let's talk about something serious. Are you single?"

My face turned rose-y, and my heart sung. I winked at him, "Not anymore, Sidney!"

Marilee chortled. "Careful Frannie, he'll take you seriously!"

Many years later, the scientific study of *Epigenetics*, which proves that trauma is passed down through three generations, would come into the mainstream. The scientific field purports that if a child is told trauma-inducing information, that child may have difficulty differentiating between whether he/she had personally survived the actual trauma or had just heard about it. *Epigenetics* also states that Holocaust survivors, as well as survivors of other forms of trauma, have passed their suffering to their children and grandchildren through their DNA. This is what I believe happened to me. Obviously, the environment I was raised in as a result of my parents suffering also damaged me. A medley of nature and nurture.

From the first time I started therapy at the Holocaust Center, in between the occasional bouts of humor, being amongst those treasured people who had similar heritage to mine had generated an uncontainable grief which seemed stored in me. Sorrow for the traditions I was robbed of and the grandparents, aunts, uncles and countless relatives who I would never know. I was furious at dad for having denied me the option of being proudly Jewish and to honor those members of my family who were murdered, not to mention the ability to get to know my living relatives.

"Such a rip-off!" I wept. "My whole childhood. Faking who I was, feeling scared almost all the time and like I'd done something wrong instead of celebrating our freedom to carry on traditions. It really messed me up."

But a few days before my twenty-third birthday, during therapy, I decided I was done with it. I knew that if I kept attending, I would keep crying for the rest of my life. I hadn't hit a comedy club once since I'd been in group. I knew that I had to stop coming to therapy. I had been too sad and I needed a comedy fix. I wasn't feeling quite ready to get back onstage, but I started writing some shtick. I didn't know what I would spew out, but I sensed it had to do with the subjects of sexuality, being raped and standing up for being Jewish. I remembered how one time a drunk on the subway had razzed me about my "Jewish nose", terrifying me into silence. I thought of a line I wished that I'd spat at him then: "Hah! You think my nose is big? You should see my clitoris!"

Momma had asked me to visit her on Friday. I intended to write more on the train ride. I was really looking forward to seeing her. Therapy had opened something up inside and made me feel more for her. The betrayal of my father while she was locked into raising me and my six brothers and sisters, and her powerful desire to be who she was by bringing customs into our home.

Chapter 45

Chopin was playing on the kitchen radio and mom was humming along. She turned to me, stroking my Cheek. "Why so much eyeliner? You look like a punk rocker!"

"Mother!"

She got up, turned off the radio, and came back to the table. "Frances, I have something important to tell you. Jah, there is no other way to say this." She squeezed my hand. "I have liver cancer."

Her face was vacant of pain, which made her words seem all that more unreal. I didn't know how to take it. I had hoped that now, since I finally understood more of what she suffered with dad, that we could get close.

"Frances, you hear me?"

My words came out staccato. "Are you sure? I mean, have you had a second opinion?"

"Yes."

"But, Momma. People survive. I mean you can get chemo. Right? Which I'm sure won't be fun. But people survive and --"

"Frances, I've researched this up and down. The chances of chemo eradicating this particular cancer are so very low. I would rather use my remaining time to feel as well as long as I can. Chemo would make me very sick."

"But, isn't there something else? Isn't it worth investigating, Mother, because what if, just what if it works?"

"The chances really are practically non-existent, Sweetheart. I want to be as well as I can for as long as I can so that I have the energy to be with my children. So many things I was robbed of teaching you because your dad sent you away. How to properly run a household. Take care of things --" She smiled at me. "I still have time."

My entire childhood, I could barely recall but there were a few times when she and I were able to feel truly close. And now here we were, finally, able to deeply connect, but with such little time left. All I could do was look at my courageous mother.

I moved closer to drape my arms around her. "Oh, Momma!"

I felt her whimper. She dabbed her eyes with her ever-ready sleeve tissue. Suddenly, she looked at her watch, then abruptly got up. "Candles!"

"What Mom?" Had she lost her noodle?

She raced to a cabinet, talking to me over her shoulder. "I'll show you the prayers another time --we're almost too late!"

"What prayers, Momma?"

She grabbed candle holders and candles, set them on top of the table, and lit them. Standing in the glow, covering her eyes, she prayed in a language I assumed was Yiddish. Afterwards, she looked at my blank face. "Hebrew, Frances." She came over and took my hands, as the flames danced in her eyes. "Frances, sit, listen. One truly wonderful thing is that I've converted back to Judaism. My brother, Gerd, oversaw everything. Was long overdue."

Just then one of the candles sparked making us jump, and then laugh. It was so odd that at the moment when I knew that my mom was dying, I finally saw her as my Jewish mom.

"We have company!" I said.

"You have no idea, Frances!" Momma laughed. "If anything can, this will give me added time." She smiled at me, and raised both fists in a gesture of victory. "This will."

She patted my hand. "Come now Shnukie, we have lots of good times left together."

"Mom, I'm so sorry that we haven't spent more time together."

"Frances, we lived together for a good year, an unexpected gift. You go on with your life now.

Succeed at what you love. That will make me happy! Now let's use this time for positive things, instead of being sad. Jah?"

I nodded slowly.

Not a second later, she tilted her chin up and peered at me from under her bifocals. "why so much eyeliner, Frances?"

"Mother! Because, that's why," I snapped, then felt bad realizing I sounded juvenile. Hastily changing the subject to something which carried more weight, I asked about Marcus. She didn't answer right away, so I knew she was editing. All she would share was that he was undergoing tests for mental health and required privacy.

Back in the big city. I decided to look for administrative work and secured a job as a corporate entertainment booking agent.

Momma phoned me one evening. She didn't call very often, so I feared a turn for the worse. She told me that she had news about Marcus, that she hadn't wanted to overload me during my visit, but that he had been diagnosed with paranoid schizophrenia, and institutionalized. He was going to be heavily medicated.

I had to slam the phone down. Institutionalized? I couldn't bear thinking about the ramifications. As I tried to unravel the nature and nurture in my life, I wondered whether the paranoia we had been raised with in our home had permeated Marcus's psyche. Or had it come through my father's DNA or a combination of both? I bought a forty-ounce bottle of vodka and drank it.

Fifteen hours later, I woke, thick with nausea. After I stopped vomiting, I listened to my phone messages. The entertainment agency was looking for me.

I had befriended a well-heeled agent at work. I decided to phone her first to tell her about Marcus. She said she had an idea that might be very helpful for him, and to meet her at her home that evening.

A few hours later, I found myself sitting in her Asian-themed living room, sipping tea. "From everything I've heard and read about psychotropic drugs, they numb you out -- eventually destroy your motor skills, your concentration. I --I'm not saying I'm healed or anything, but I went to group therapy for a while, and it helped me to realize that I'm actually not all that crazy! I really feel what my brother needs is to be surrounded by emotionally healthy people who can you know…train him to redirect his thoughts and feelings. Re-brainwash him if you will. Instead of zapping him with drugs. He's a piano prodigy."

My friend Pam explained that she had an heiress friend whose schizophrenic son inspired her to finance a cutting-edge program which used powerful supplements, as opposed to psychotropic drugs, together with emotional and cerebral retraining. It had an enormous success rate in Europe. Her son had triumphed. Pam had already told her about Marcus, and she said she'd be happy to help.

I continued to thank her as she dialed her friend, then introduced us.

"Is it safe?" I asked the heiress.

"We have round-the-clock personal security as well as twenty-four-hour on-call therapists. This system has already been lauded by many allopathic doctors in Europe, helping schizophrenics transition from psychotropic medication to a regimen of super-powered vitamins, combined with intensive personalized restructuring of negative patterns or derisive thoughts that many schizophrenics have. My boy has improved significantly and is almost entirely independent."

"Is it expensive?"

"I am in a position to take your brother with absolutely no charge. What I need is a letter with a few signatures from family members, in case of an accident. Highly unlikely, since he will have a security guard with him at all times, including in the bathroom and shower."

"Thank you so much! I-I don't know what to say." My heart raced as I imagined Marcus's expression after being released from psychic lock-up. He could eventually pursue training for a career as a musician. Maybe, one day I could even convince him to move to Toronto and be my neighbor. Yahoo! This was his ticket out of *Crazyville*! And honestly, I was petrified that his diagnosis would have a dreadful impact on my own mental health. What if dad was right about me?

I phoned mom, breathlessly relaying the news. I told her that I was sending her a letter of support which required her signature as well as those from as many Sheridan's as possible. I knew that trying to get my dad onboard was futile.

"Fantastic, Frances! A real miracle!" she said, her voice filled with glee.

Two days later, Momma phoned to tell me that she had changed her mind. That her doctor had convinced her that putting Marcus on the heiress's program, no matter how highly supervised, was too dangerous.

"I know this is hard to accept, Frances," she said softly "but your brother will be well cared for.

At least he will be sufficiently sedated not to take his own life! Perhaps an institution for a short while, but then a nice group home."

Nice group home? How could she! He didn't have to kill himself; they were doing it for him. I felt completely stripped of my ballast. Grasping for something, I phoned Diddy to test his reaction.

"I am sorry Frannie, but that is your brother's reality! Just be thankful that I got you away from your mother in time, with her Jewish nonsense. Very dangerous wishy-washy behavior! Be careful of her Frannie, your brother didn't know which way to turn his head. But I will always have a room for you in Vienna, with your own desk, waiting for you when you are ready. I send you a big fatherly hug all the way from Vienna!"

Rather than fatherly arms, a straitjacket would soon be hugging Marcus. How could Diddy be so laissez-faire about his own son? I felt eviscerated. Dad had said for ages that Marcus and I were crazy in different ways. But now that this was happening to him, I believed that it might be true and it could happen to me too. I felt lost. I started to question my own paranoia with standup. Paranoia here, paranoia there, paranoia everywhere.

Chapter 46

I went to visit mother several times over the next few months. I pushed aside my feelings about what she'd said about Marcus. She wasn't showing signs of deterioration yet.

One day, Marcus dropped by. His eyes were glazed and he had gained weight. He chronically moved the fingers of one hand. I didn't want to embarrass him by asking but determined it was a medication side-effect. He had spent several months in a mental health institution. He was now living in a boarding home. Mother had become a board member of an organization geared towards helping those with mental health issues to secure accommodation. They visited each other every week. She made sure that he was in excellent hands and would continue to be after she had gone.

One day when the three of us were riding the elevator in the building where Momma lived, heading back to her condo, Marcus began to babble. "I hate it when people look at me with lop-sided lips!"

"Well, maybe you are misinterpreting them, Marcus!" I clamored for words.

"No, I can feel their disgust with me. And I understand it!" said Marcus.

"Well, I love it when people look at me!" said Momma, shamelessly proud. "It means they think I look nice. And I do!"

I smooched Momma's cheek. I wondered if I liked it when people looked at me? I mean, I knew I liked the attention but when I thought about it I particularly enjoyed it when people really saw the real me underneath.

Later that day, she told me that over the years, she had reached out to my dad, in an attempt to reconcile. He had consistently refused to communicate. But now, having received word about her illness through someone in the family, he had expressed a desire to come to see her. She had rejected his request to say goodbye, and possibly to seek forgiveness.

I was happy that in her eleventh hour, she had finally taken the reins. I know that she had never stopped loving him.

A few months later, I received a phone call from a nurse. Mom had been admitted to a Palliative Care unit. The nurse suggested, strongly, that I visit.

When I walked into Momma's room, she was on a morphine drip, all bones and jaundiced skin. A nurse was smiling softly, attempting to feed her. I kissed mother's cheek and squeezed her gnarled hand.

She turned to me, attempting to speak, but only emitted a throaty noise.

"You must be the baby girl," the nurse said warmly. "I'm Bella."

I swallowed my emotions. "Frannie, Yep."

"We were expecting you. I've been taking care of your sweet mother for a few weeks now --"

"Weeks? I had no--" mom grunted at Bella, who then passed me a notepad.

"When your mother was first admitted, she had me write this for you to read upon your arrival."

Momma watched carefully, as I sat on the bed and read the note out loud. "What would you like?" I knew she meant which of her things would I like to inherit, but I said, "For you to get better, my beautiful Mother! Enough of this kidding around, already!"

I smiled and stroked her hand, which was covered with the liver spots. Before Momma's illness, I had thought they looked beautiful, like enlarged happy freckles. But now set against a yellowed background, they appeared garish.

Bella took the untouched tray. "I'll leave you two alone. Press the button if you need me."

Mom reached for my hand with great effort, imploring me. I looked at her but said nothing. A big tear rolled down her cheek, dismantling my armor, and we cried together. "Momma, you're getting me all mushy." I took a few gigantic breaths, trying to control my sobs. I didn't have to think twice. "Okay, okay, your housecoat,

Momma. That's what I want, your housecoat." She nodded at me, knowingly. She had worn the orange and red-flowered housecoat heaps of times when cuddling me.

The day of Momma's funeral was hideously rainy and cold, as if the scene had been set in an over-the-top B-movie. All of us kids squished inside one limo, along with Uncle Gerd. I brought everyone a small box of tissues as well as a rose. As nice as it was to see my siblings, I wasn't able to take much in. Nobody was speaking. Swollen-eyed and spent, I searched out the window for a distraction. I wondered if dad knew Momma was about to be buried. I imagined him feeling full of regret.

Uncle Gerd turned to look at me, his eyes misted. "I haven't seen you since you were a little girl, Frannie. You are the image of your mother."

I tried to smile but erupted in unstoppable sobs which continued to flow until the car stilled at the side of the road, next to a cemetery marked with a large Star-of-David sculpture.

The next day, I awoke on the comfy velvet sectional in mother's living room. I had cried so much, the sockets of my eyes were parched. Momma's housecoat which she had promised to me, was draped over the back of the sofa. I buried my nose in its soft padding, instantly drunk on Momma's still-lingering scent.

My siblings had already gone to their respective lodgings which were located in different parts of North America. I knew that some of them kept in touch with each other more than they did with me. It tugged at me a little, but so much time had passed since we'd been close that they felt a little bit like strangers. We had promised to see each other more often, but I knew that was doubtful.

Chapter 47

At 5:00 a.m., I awoke from a gluey state in the room above the strip club. I'd been dreaming about trying to piece together a brightly colored abstract sculpture of my family but chunks had kept falling off.

Standing up in the walk-in freezer that served as my room, my flesh was too cold to feel the full post-stripping ache throbbing inside every muscle in my legs, but they still smarted. The muscle relaxants had worn off.

The marquee outside the hotel flashed on and off, sporadically illuminating my worn-out room, which could have been a cover photo for a *Good Housekeeping* Horror magazine. I forced myself to walk through the sludgy carpet to the window. Lacey snowflakes fell, immediately losing their magic when reaching the flickering sign of a naked female figure that read *Girls! Girls! Girls!,* merely resembling dandruff on a neon hooker.

I flicked on the light switch. Searing beams from a single 150-watt bulb dangling from an exposed wire practically caused my dry eyeballs to pucker. I brewed a pot of unexpectedly decent instant hotel room coffee, heaping in the sugar.

Fondling the soft chapbook cover of my play, I flipped open the first few pages to where it read 'Published by International Readers Theater, copyright 1997'. Even though I had now been working as a stripper for six weeks, seeing my past accomplishments in print gave me hope that there were better things to come. The play had been well received from the moment I first started performing it in 1995, just a mere four years ago, I reminded myself. I could almost still feel the thrill of the audience response.

I had named it *The Waltonsteins*, a sendup of the title of the 70's TV series *The Waltons* which was about a large, happy gentile family whose son was called John-boy. We Sheridans weren't happy, we weren't Gentiles, and my eldest brother could only have been referred to as *A Jew-boy*.

Chapter **48**

Touring across the country performing my irreverent feminist standup comedy act, often to terrific reviews, was sporadically interrupted by my old stress disorder monster. Still, I pushed ahead. I positioned a bit in the middle of my act that touched on the ridiculousness of people pretending to be something they so obviously aren't -- politicians pretending to be human beings, for example. And then for a moment I felt fearless. In that instant I shared how my Jewish parents had raised me Catholic but were so clearly Jewish. I disclosed that when we attended church, dad used to complain all the way through communion.

Hunching my shoulders, I spoke in a Yiddish-European accent, "I can't eat this cracker, it's so dry…needs a shmear of pickled herring…something, a little cream cheese, vat is this?!"

The audience screamed with laughter. It was like receiving a combination of an absolution and an orgasm.

I kept the bit in my show. Although my heart would always race right before I delivered the lines, it was riveting to share my scariest secret and receive such consistently positive responses. The genie was out of the bottle and I was pulled to dig deeper into writing about my heritage.

One sleepless night after performing standup in Vancouver, I felt compelled to call my father to tell him that I wanted to transform our family story into a live performance. I wanted to let him know that truth-telling in a comedy club to a warm audience had felt like a baptism of free-speech water. That I wasn't suggesting that I now had "tell-it-like-it-is-itis" and would speak my mind in situations I sensed weren't going to serve me, but that there were times when being honest was less of a risk to my well-being than living a lie. That I could no longer live my life feeling like I was trapped inside my head. I intended to tell him that I knew how scared he was and that my heart broke for him. But that as his child I had something burning in me to move his story out of the darkness so that we could stop hiding and begin to heal.

"How dare you --I will take you to court!" Diddy growled, "You're placing yourself and our family in grave danger! You cannot write someone's story without their written permission!"

I slammed down the phone. But the words "tell your story, tell your story" swam in my head again. I couldn't relax, couldn't move ahead, couldn't sleep. I wrote tirelessly, spewing out endless pages of dark stories about my childhood.

I didn't have a clear vision as to how I would create a show, so I began sniffing out the path. I asked around for referrals for a director and found Jessica Van Der Veen. She immediately fell in love with the story. I decided to settle in Vancouver.

Jess led me to physically impersonate everyone who I'd written about in the play. I improvised the stories transforming them into powerful scenes. Eight weeks later we mounted a performance at a hundred-seat venue called Gastown Theater.

On opening night, I sat at my make-up table, taking in photographs of my parents and my grandparents which I brought for courage and inspiration. "Speak through me" I whispered.

The stage manager startled me with a loud rap on my dressing room door. "Places Frannie!"

Everything in me tightened and my mind filled with dread. *Was I really going to do this…publicly out my entire family? Was this worth endangering us? Was I crazy?*

I willed myself to ascend the stairs leading to the stage. But once I reached the landing, the spirit of my maternal grandmother Selma Zwienicki, the one who had been murdered on Kristallnacht, made her existence known to me. I hadn't been thinking of her but suddenly I felt her presence. I sensed a different vibration and it was as if she was telling me "It's time to tell the story for all of us".

"Speak through me," I whispered, emboldened to walk onstage.

Afterwards, the audience was transfixed. A journalist named David Spanner who had been in the crowd wrote about my family story and work in the internationally published magazine *The Jerusalem Report*. I received very moving phone calls from extended relatives who had read the article. They had been searching for our family for forty-five years, ever since my dad had gone undercover as a Catholic, cutting off ties with all extended family.

Although Jess and I had created a wonderful theatrical telling, I wanted to strengthen the show. I felt that amongst other things it needed a theatrical spine, a storyline to hang the scenes on which would take the audience on a ride while the story unfolded. I began working with Lynna Goldhar-Smith, who in addition to being a playwright and director, incorporated musical scoring and lighting which brought an additional dimension to plays.

We rewrote the play together, theatricalizing my crippling anxiety by having me escape from an abusive character who we named my "Little Friend". Being a one-person show, I played both parts, whirling around onstage as I transitioned from one character to the other. We dramatized the discovery of my familial secrets by having me mime taking a train ride back to my childhood home, where I then moved from room to room, uncovering mysteries and memories.

The reviews were stellar. Following the nightly standing ovation at The Norman Rothstein Theater, the show always ended as I recalled a happy memory: Impersonating my father, I danced and sang and mimed playing the violin under the beautiful golden maple tree in our backyard. But before the curtains closed, I would always share the following with the audience:

"My father has some very happy memories of his life in Vienna before the Second World War --there were over nine million Jews living in Europe. They lived in villages, towns, cities, out in the countryside -- they were everywhere. In Poland, Estonia, in Germany, Latvia, Lithuania, Austria, Greece, Holland, Hungary, France, Belgium, Yugoslavia, Romania, Czechoslovakia, the Ukraine. After the war…in most of those countries eighty-five percent, ninety percent gone! Vanished! Disappeared! Murdered, burned, gassed, shot, starved, tortured. Men, women, children, babies, mothers, brothers, sisters, grandparents. Lost. Lost forever. No graves, no monuments. Gone. Over thirty-five million people died in this terrible, terrible war. Soldiers, political prisoners, dissidents, homosexuals, gypsies. It is beyond imagining. It is beyond understanding...all of this death. This terrible, terrible ordeal. It is beyond forgetting. There is no forgetting this. Only one third of the Jews escaped death at the hands of the Nazis -- my parents were among these and I...I am proud of them. They were brave. They survived. So why is this my legacy, all of this fear and shame? I won't accept this inheritance. I am claiming my own inheritance. I want to celebrate their courage and I want to say it loud! I am a Jew!"

Chapter 49

A few days later, Lynna and I were sitting in her comfy colorful home toasting to our success. I had come over to share some exciting news. I eyed a copy of one of our favorite write-ups about the play which was lying on her coffee table. It was a stunning nine-page feature article written by journalist Shelley Page and published in the national Canadian paper *The Ottawa Citizen*. Shelley had flown to Vienna to interview Dad, to Tucson to have a discussion with Madalen and had also received opinions from Philip and other family members.

"So, what's the big news?" Lynna asked, pouring me a refill of fruity burgundy.

I pointed to the article. "Shelley phoned me. She said that the film director Arthur Hiller --you know he directed like fifty-million movies *The Man in The Glass Booth* I watched when I was a teen-ager…but anyway, Shelley said that he read her article."

"Okay, okay…that's exciting, but I'm dying to know the bottom line!" said Lynna excitedly sensing that there was more to the story…

"Well, you remember in Shelley's piece, she alluded to my having written a screenplay based on my family story?"

Lynna nodded.

"Okay, so Shelley tells me that Arthur has been calling Ottawa to look for me because he assumed I still lived there. So, they gave him my telephone number here. And she said he'd be phoning. At first, I thought that she was playing a prank. But Lynna, a few minutes after she and I ended the call, his assistant phoned."

Lynna's mouth fell open.

"So, he asked if I would send him my screenplay for his consideration? I was like…yeah, I think that would be okay, Mr. Hiller!"

"Come on!" she said rolling her big brown eyes.

"I'm totally serious!"

"No way! *The* Arthur Hiller? The guy who directed the brilliant film *Love Story*, with a resume longer than that porn star --Ron Jeremy's *shmekel* --penis?"

I roared. "Classy reference, Lynna! But yep. And he wants me to send him the screenplay I co-wrote with Pat Bermel," I said referring to a talented writer friend who I had penned the first draft of the script with.

"Wow!" Lynna was speechless.

"It's un-real, Lynna! We created this - this momentum together!"

She smiled. "Thanks, Frannie. That means a lot. Usually, people think that all a director does is move a chair onstage."

The effects of the play snowballed. It was produced in Ottawa, the city of my birth, by Temple Israel, a synagogue who united together with St. Basil's church, the congregation that we Sheridan's had attended as Catholics. After having read Shelley's phenomenal article, both the temple administrator Heather Cohen, and the head priest from the church, Father Corbin Eddy, individually phoned me, wanting to book the play. I suggested that they co-produce. It turned out to be the first time that the two communities connected, inspiring much healing.

Following my performance in front of a packed house of 900 at the stunning Museum of Civilization Theater, during a Question-and-Answer period, Arthur Hiller came to stand in front of the microphone. The audience gasped recognizing him as the president of the Academy of Arts and Sciences, from the countless times he had introduced the Academy Awards. It took me a few moments to take in the grandiosity of the moment. For a moment I remembered that both the Jewish and Catholic communities were sitting together in the audience like one big family. It felt like the true meaning of communion. Seconds later, I was once again awestruck by Mr. Hiller's famous Semitic profile. He had flown in to surprise me from his home in Beverly Hills. He announced that he had read the screenplay and was interested in turning it into a film.

"We'll speak afterwards," he said. I nodded, unable to shut my mouth.

My siblings had come to Ottawa to watch me impersonate them. That alone cost me twelve sessions of therapy. But their attendance was priceless, as well as that of in-laws, nieces and nephews, some of whom I'd never met.

Afterwards, Madalen took my hand and said "Frannie, if you do nothing else as an artist, you've done enough. I'm so proud of you."

I held her tight, trying not to cry. As an adult, it was such a gift to receive those words from her, particularly because dad had pitted us against each other by placing us on opposing sides of our family.

Chapter 50

On the flight back to Vancouver, Lynna sensed that I was distracted. I shared my concern about my finances. Even though I had a nice-sized check from my gig in my purse, it would only carry me so far. She attempted to fuel me by reminding me of some of the splendid highlights from the performance, encouraging me to trust that word-of-mouth would travel and that bookings would roll in as a result.

"To continued great success!" she toasted me with coffee. "And by the way, if rent is too much of an issue, you are welcome to be a guest in my home for as long as you want."

I hugged her. "Wow! So generous of you, Lynna! Thank you. I just wish I could nail an audition. But by the way, last week when I read for the Lottery commercial --you remember I shot one earlier this year? Anyway, Diana was in town from Brighton and we read for the same role...I told her about my idea to work as a stripper."

"I told you before, you could rake it in as a stripper!" nodded Lynna.

"Yeah, I appreciate your support, but it's a pretty rad option for this well-behaved Jewish gal!"

Lynna and I both "oy'd" at the same time.

We high-five'd and I continued talking. "Anyway, Diana said that it's actually a very common female fantasy -- I mean honestly, the idea of it, y'know, sharing one of the most forbidden things about myself sexually in public and getting away with it does feel sort of sexy." I tossed my head causing my dark curls to bounce. "I dunno Lynna, maybe I could, y'know, wear a wig. Adopt a different persona -- really, it'd be a solo acting job. Diana said she would help me with a British accent. I'd create a whole new identity instead of the one my dad made me adopt. The stripper versus the Catholic! What sounds like more fun?"

Lynna laughed. I kept going. "Really, it's the most shame-imbued thing I can think of that I would be willing to try -- scary, but plausible. Like, I would never consider y'know, working as a hooker. The thought of touching someone for money feels icky to me. But dancing naked is just a fantasy. It would get me close to the fire without it singeing me. And maybe, just maybe it'll melt my shame skin for good, because once I'm naked, I suspect that I'll also feel like I don't have to hide anything emotionally anymore. It's just a sense but, Lynna...I'm not sure how else to get off the shame-guilt-fear-anxiety merry-go-round? And I'm just so damn tired of feeling like I need to modulate something about myself to be acceptable and stand on my head to please people."

"I fully get it, Frannie. Although...standing on your head half-naked if you decide to strip could be pretty hot!"

"True. But at least it'd be my call. "

Lynna nodded. I kept talking. "My goal is to not care about anyone else's scrutiny on each and every level. I know it will free me."

"You're right, Frannie! But hardly anyone gets there. I say go for it, girl!"

"Thanks, Lynna. Besides, some of my favorite peeps aren't universally loved. Gandhi, Madonna, The Roadrunner..."

Lynna smiled, "Exactly. He was so annoying with that beep-beep!"

"And yet, it took him places!" I added. "Who knows, maybe I won't even end up stripping if I book this job."

"Oh, stop being so hard on yourself! You just shot a guest star spot on *The Unprofessionals* a few months ago, you did that indie a coupla weeks ago. And what about all those gigs working as an opening act for that YukYuks comic David what's-his-name --"

"Bruce. Anyway. Lynna, I had fun, but I mean something that pays consistently well! I-I just thought that once I'd done *The Waltonsteins*, that I'd be cured!"

"What are you talking about?"

"I keep blowing auditions. I just -- still, sometimes --get so freaked out, I can't stop my heart from racing, sometimes I do great but then I --"

"You'll get there, Frannie. It took years to get the way you are, be patient with your healing. You're very gifted."

"Well, you're very sweet."

"Actually, I'm not!" she chortled, flashing her sparkling brown eyes. "You know how much I hate small talk. I'm just being honest."

"I like what you do in your standup act. Y'know, if it was socially acceptable to imitate blowing your brains out," Lynna said, then imitated a 'small-talker'; "I mowed the lawn today and then I had my hair done". Then, Lynna mimed pointing a gun at her head and made a poof sound, causing me to laugh.

"Exactly! Anyway, the play is the most powerful thing I have to offer. It's like ha-ha the Nazis didn't win! Every other job feels --vacuous. I'm going to move the play to the next level and bring in some moola to produce it myself, if necessary."

"You will succeed, Frannie. Look, I know you come from the right side of the tracks, so you think you're gonna go to hell if you strip. And I'm not advocating stripping as a long-term sideline, but the truth is that although some of those girls are addicts, many are just athletes that just want to make a chunk of change with their talent. You studied jazz-ballet for years…just look at it like a great workout. Just do it for a coupla' months, you can always stop. You'll make a bucket of dough. Way more than any of the menial labor jobs you've done in between gigs. You won't become a crusty, harsh person, Frannie. You know who you really are!"

"Yeah, I guess I just don't always remember!"

Comedy Club Palm Beach 2018

People often ask me, "Being a nice Jewish girl raised Catholic, how could you justify being a stripper?" Please, Jewish and Catholic? That's like a double whammy of guilt, shame and fear --ya gotta resort to drastic measures when you're in that condition and stripping was therapy on steroids! I mean, I was so guilt-ridden in Catholic school I actually got kicked out because okay, in Home Ec we had to make dolls of Jesus being crucified but because I'm Jewish, I felt so guilty hearing that Jews killed him,

to make myself feel better I made a suicidal Jesus doll. He was holding an empty bottle of sleeping pills and downing a bottle Manischevitz…but, just a heads up; this does not make a good Christmas present for Christians!

So listen, since this is kind of a confessional, I'm gonna share one of my favorite quotes -- it's written by a Marine who said; "You'll always find religion in a fox-hole." Y'know, I have affluent religious friends super comfy with their lives but that's only because it's never been tested -- but lemmetellya, the second they're faced with a catastrophe, they are questioning the fairness of God. And when you come back from hell, you have a much greater appreciation of every little thing. So how can I justify having been a stripper? Well, instead of coming out of the womb at 'day 1', I did it at 'year thirty-nine', when I was birthed from a strip club fully naked yet feeling utterly safe. I finally got that everything is perceptual. So I enjoyed even more all that good stuff that followed.

Chapter 51

While placing the copy of my play *The Waltonsteins* back on the windowsill of the strip club hotel room, I was hit by the smell of mildew. I took a quick sniff of the cover. It wasn't the chapbook. Still, instead of returning it to its spot on the ledge, I decided to toss it into my suitcase. It made me feel better knowing that I would be taking it with me, out of the dank hotel room.

I started to get a headache from the clammy aroma. Then I realized that in a shivery moment, I had absent-mindedly wrapped my shoulders in the sleeping bag without remembering its fungus-infused stench. I threw it into a corner of the room, then plopped down in my suitcase. Fondling the soft-covered copy of the play, I recalled the encouraging pep talk Lynna had given me before I started working as a stripper. And now, I couldn't wait to tell her about that first moment onstage when I had realized how safe I felt standing fully nude, I was so unexpectedly comfortable in my skin that I almost laughed out loud. I wouldn't have cared less if someone had boo'd at any perceived physical imperfections, or at my kooky prop humor. The audience's acceptance of my basic nakedness, my scariest performance ever, was deeply warming. Whoddathunkit? Not the morality squad, that's for sure. But what if the audience had been in a bad mood? It occurred to me that every opinion about everything was really just a reflection of the judgers emotional state. "Who cares what people think?" I heard myself say out loud.

At last, the world seemed more interesting in its diversity then threatening. Sure, it would involve practicing a sustained effort to be able to maintain my optimistic direction. Lynna had rightly said that since it had taken me years to get screwy, I needed to be patient with my healing, but I felt strongly that I could retrain myself. I knew that I could learn to focus on feeling positive about myself more consistently. Nothing was wrong with me naked or clothed and never had been. I was sure of that now. All that prior negative judgement was just me buying into someone else's twisted bad feelings. Like dad had, and then passed those crappy feelings, and his practiced behavior onto me. Poor Diddy! He had just lost his focus.

The pipes crackled in my hotel room. After six weeks I'd had enough of the freezing weather not to mention the sex-infused environment. My hand grazed the icy windowpane. I breathed hot air on it and rubbed a clear spot. I could see an empty car lot past the marquee of naked girls. Even though it was still dark outside, I decided to head out to use a pay phone located down the street to check my voicemail.

I pulled a hat over my red wig and headed down to the lobby. Two bikers smoking a joint nodded as I walked by.

Opening the door, the assault of air was so fresh and cold that it hurt my lungs.

I dialed my number. Three messages. The first was a positive response to a writing grant I'd applied for. Five thousand dollars. I "yahoo'd" and "Thank you'd" out loud, forgetting my phony British accent, creating puffs in the crystal clear, icy air. Luckily, the street was deserted.

My second message was from a radio producer informing me that a radio documentary based on my play, also called *The Waltonsteins*, which had been broadcast in Canada and the states as part of a CBC/NPR exchange had won an esteemed award for excellence in broadcasting called The Gabriel.

My third message was from Diddy. I heard him whimper and then there was dead air. Had he dialed me, then realized that he was ill, too sick to speak? Was he alone? Should I contact my older siblings about going to Vienna to see him? Then, he sobbed. My breath caught. "I don't like being alone here. Ghosts, ghosts, everybody murdered. The buildings hold the memories --you can

---

http://www.cbc.ca/andthewinneris/2013/05/06/the-waltensteins/

feel it. I miss my parents. Beautiful people. Once, in the middle of the night, they were really here, not just ghosts. They came to see me in human form, if only for an instant. I could feel my Momma's hand. I needed to find out what happened to them, Frances. I went to the *Wiesenthal Center* and --"

Then all I heard were noises. I knew that Diddy had covered the receiver with his hand so that I wouldn't hear him spilling more tsunami-sized waves of grief.

He continued. "They were taken in a train load and shot at the side of the road, by what the Nazis called helpful Lithuanians. A mass grave. I was one day too late when I came back to Vienna looking for them. The earth, it doesn't forget, Frances. Even a rock has a soul. Even a small stone. Every night --"

The answering machine cut him off. I was crying too hard to listen anyway. Then the answering machine played the next message. It was Diddy again. I took a huge breath and wiped my face with the icy sleeve of my parka.

"Every night, I sleep on the floor here, whispering to my Momma so that I can be near. I press my cheek down and kiss the ground they walked on --sometimes they feel so near. Once, I see a light go on in the kitchen. I tell you they were here, Frances."

"You did everything you could, Diddy," I found myself saying to his recorded voice. My heart literally hurt from the weight of his sadness. I could hear that he was still talking but I couldn't take listening to his tortuous stories any longer. I had been the recipient of far too many of his tales of horror. I hung up, trying to calm my sobs. A car drove by causing me to look up. My vision was blurry from the nonstop streams of hot tears, but I could see that the sun was starting to rise. The pedestrian traffic would be picking up soon, and I didn't feel like speaking with anyone, phony British accent or not. I took a few breaths, rubbed my eyes and willed myself to phone back to listen to the rest of Daddy's message so I could scurry back to the room afterwards. As shaken as I was by his nonstop grief. I missed him terribly.

I redialed my voicemail, then fast-forwarded to the place in the message where I had stopped listening. He continued, "I know you think I am terrible for what I've done to our family --I read the play reviews --but I only know what I lived and what I saw.

There is no safe place for a Jew. Israel, surrounded by people who think they get a ticket to heaven to kill us? I didn't want to put my children in that danger, Frances. But you my daughter, because of your play, have given me the courage to finally return to my roots, which I had never left in my heart. Yesterday, I publicly revoked my Catholicism and officially redeclared myself a Jew at the Jewish Community Center here in Vienna. Today, I bought a plot in the Jewish Central Cemetery in the Jewish section. If you come to visit me after I'm gone, it is walking distance to the grave of my grand-dad Rabbi Izi Hirsch Beutel, the only marked grave of a relative." Then he sighed. "So..." he paused. I knew that he was trying to calm himself.

I paused playback. What? I was beyond stunned. Had I heard right? I had to hear it again. It was delicious, but I couldn't entirely take it in. It was too awesome, too startling. I replayed that segment of his voicemail. It was real! I paused the message, wishing that Momma was with me to share the wonder.

"Wow, wow, wow!" I shouted out loud. I didn't care if anyone had heard. Just then an owl came and sat on top of the half-roof that covered the open phone booth. My mouth fell open. We both stared at each other. I had never seen an owl up close. I felt strongly that I was being given a message from Momma and that she was very much with me, with us. I smiled and at that moment, it flew away. My breathing returned to normal. I continued to listen to the rest of Diddy's message.

"The theater show you make is interesting to this film director, Arthur Hiller? This is the elegant gentleman with the mane of hair, who announced the Academy Awards each year on television, jah? Well Sweetheart, pick up the phone and call your old Diddy when you get a --" then the machine went dead, so I hung up. My eyelids were swollen from crying so hard. Even in the freezing air they burned. But I felt as if my father had given me an enormous present. For so long I had wanted him to be happy, longing for him to find a way to recover how proud he had once been of being Jewish. And although I knew that it was doubtful that in this lifetime, he would ever be entirely free of emotional bondage, I felt so good that he had miraculously acknowledged that my Jewish pride-in-identity work had *sechel*--soul.

Although I was spent, I was bubbling with joy. My fragmented father had returned to me with an unexpected piece intact.

As I reentered the strip club, the irony hit me. After working in an exotic dance nightclub where I had gotten stark naked, which surprisingly helped me to discover a way to concentrate my feelings so that I no longer required anyone else's stamp of approval in order to feel good, I had finally received an emotional endorsement from my father. I wasn't a nutcase after all! I decided that it was time to vacate my sideline.

The management was agreeable regarding my departure. I went to my room, packed, and then made my way downstairs to the front door, a thick wad of cash in my wallet, and wigless.

A biker was positioned at the front desk, acting as a bouncer. I had previously only revealed myself to him as *SmartiePanties* and in full drag.

He did a double take. "Holy shit!"

"It's real!" I said shaking my curls.

"I much prefer it to that road-kill you were wearing!" he joked.

I smiled, proud to be flaunting my Yiddish curls. He called a taxi, then carried my bags to the car. I thanked him, sat in the back, shut the door and opened the window. "Hey!" I yelled to him, just as he was re-entering the hotel. He turned around. "I have one other thing to tell you."

He cocked an eyebrow.

"I'm not really --"

"You're not really --what?" He waited, then his expression darkened. "Oh fuck, don't tell me you're a guy!"

"No, no." I laughed. Then I dropped my British accent. "I'm not really British!"

He looked terribly confused. "Drive! Bus station!" I commanded to the befuddled-looking driver while rolling up the window. *I did it, I did it, I did it!*

Epilogue

Iblame Madonna's '90's music for helping to infuse me with an even greater sense of sexual fun. I blared her music for hours during my time off, while on the road touring my play *The Waltonsteins*. In 1997, 'Take A Bow' was released. It held many meanings for me. Not only was I performing my play to receptive international crowds, I was also putting on quite a show in the sack. I wasn't simply dating one person, I was simultaneously seeing both a Catholic and a Jewish guy. I know what you're thinking. No, I wasn't *shtupping* (for the Yiddish-challenged that means sleeping with them) at the same time in the same bed. Different beds, different times. But you must understand that it marked a milestone in my healing; having inherited post-traumatic stress disorder from my parents, decades earlier when I first became romantically involved it was always very trying for my partner because I spent more time sleeping under the bed than on it.

But as I had gotten over my discomfort years ago, and being a romantic at heart, now juggling two guys felt off. They had both professed their love for me and I them, but we hadn't discussed monogamy. It's not that I felt guilty. I knew that women feel guiltier than men when it came to the number of their sexual conquests. You still hear the female lament; "I should have waited!" But how often do you hear a guy say, "I wish I hadn't slept with her --I feel like such a slut!" Exactly. And having been raised Jewish and Catholic I had the option to give up guilt for Lent! Still, I wanted to close on one, but they both had equal pros and negs. The Catholic was buff, blue-collar, with a good career in film production but loved licking the rolling paper for his joints more than my *shmushmu*, whereas the paunchy, well-educated, camel-eyed Jew who would devour me as if I was lying on a bed of truffles, freelanced intermittently as a documentary producer. I cared about them equally and like an idiot, had given them their own keys.

My darling friend Diana who had engineered my Brighton accent during my short foray as a stripper, had moved to Vancouver from England. She was renting an apartment in a high-rise located next door to my second-floor walk-up. As it turned out, her balcony allowed for a birds' eye view of my back door. One day in between touring, as Moishe and I made out in between mouthfuls of moo shoo pork, the phone rang. Being a religious guy, eating the forbidden food during sex was for him a form of Jewish S&M.

I ignored the phone, captivated by his head-hanging which he interspersed with sighs of pleasure. A moment later, it rang again. I picked up the receiver.

"Frannie, get out of the apartment immediately!" Diana screeched. "The pope is coming up your back stairs right now! I saw you going into your place about twenty minutes ago with the rabbi. Get out of there now!" she shouted, using the monikers we had previously established for my current boyfriends.

"Oh God, thanks!" I hung up and pushed the Jew out the front door mid-chew, locking it just as Patrick the Catholic opened the back door. I knew I had to terminate one of the relationships before getting busted by my suitors, who then might want to terminate me.

After much mulling, I recognized that I was actually more pulled to be with the forbidden fruit, Moishe.

A few hours later, I unlocked the door to my apartment, intent on ending things with Patrick. I was momentarily seduced by the aroma of chicken pie baking. It was his mother's recipe and my fav.

"Angel, let me pour you a glass of wine!" he trilled from the kitchen, then met me in the hall where he kissed me, and handed me a glass of my favorite merlot.

"Wow! You're amazing, Patrick!" I said, moving past him to the kitchen.

He tailed me into the kitchen. We toasted and I took an enormous gulp. I peeked at the pie through the oven door window. "Patrick, you are so sweet and..." I continued slowly, looking away from him, trying to sense the best words to end our union.

"You really are," I continued. "The nicest guy on really every level. Which is why I'm being honest with you."

"I should hope so," he intoned provocatively, folding me into his arms.

"Do you know how when, um..."

He kissed me passionately. "Y'wanna tell me this in there?" he intoned, motioning to the bedroom.

I disentangled myself from him. "Patrick, sit. I need you to listen."

"Yes Ma'am!" he teased, saluting.

Damn, did he have to be so charming?

"So, y'know when gay people have been closeted they come out and understandably want to be with other gay people, right?"

His eyes widened "Are you gay, babe? That's fine with me --as a matter of fact we could make it work well. The idea of two women --"

"Stop! I'm not gay, Patrick. I'm Jewish."

"Oh, now you tell me!" he joked. "Damn! I had this stripping Nazi thing planned for you but I guess I should just return the Wehrmacht uniform to 'Costume World'!"

I hated that he made me laugh. He always did. "Listen Adolf, we have to stop seeing each other! For real, Patrick. I feel the same way gay people do when they come out. I told you my story before --I came out of the *knish* closet, so I really just want to be...with a Jew."

Patrick banged his wine glass on the table. The burgundy alcohol spilled onto the white linen tablecloth I'd inherited from mom. "That's racist!"

"If you take it out of context...but it's actually a normal yearning. At least if you've been denied being with your own kind. Cats want to be with cats, and..."

"Give me a break!" he huffed.

I took his hand, but he pulled it away. "Patrick, listen! In the same way that a First Nations person, stolen from their community and forced into a Christian upbringing is drawn to be with another indigenous Indian, having been raised to suppress my Jewish self, I feel similarly. Would you rather I strung you along, Patrick? I just realized this. You are the greatest guy --you know I feel that way, and --"

"This is bullshit!" he roared. "I'm outta here. Enjoy the fuckin' pie!"

And with that, he left. I knew that I had made the right decision for myself but felt horrible that I hurt him. So to take the edge off, being a Jew, I devoured the whole pie, and washed it down with a pint of chocolate chip ice cream.

Moishe was more amorous than ever, delighting in being my "chosen one". But as Arthur Hiller became more involved in creating press for the film he intended to direct, based on my play, Moishe began shooting nasty comments at me. I realized that he was jealous. And, as media interest grew, I was interviewed for national television and radio about my play and impending movie project.

One day while Moishe and I sat eating popcorn in a movie theater, the trailer for an upcoming indie film festival was being shown. I had been featured in the role of the actress. Seeing my face on the big screen caused him to shout with ferocity, "Oh, give me a break!"

After Moishe's public announcement, I privately announced to him that I needed more "variety" in my life, which would no longer include him. As much as I yearned for a romantic Jewish partner, I was clear that I wanted to be with someone who would not only be comfortable sharing the limelight but would feel proud if I occasionally shone brighter in the public eye.

That same day, the journalist Army Archerds' piece entitled 'Hiller Works on Waltonsteins' had come out in *Variety* magazine. Seeing the words in print moved me to tears: "The father was so paranoid about the holocaust, and what happened to its children, he and his wife and the children converted to Catholicism in Canada. How they regained their identity and the participation of the Catholic Church in their reconversion are parts of the drama. Hiller learned of the story when it was being performed in a one-woman show in Ottawa by Frannie Sheridan." Having my work celebrated by such a prominent Jewish director flooded me with joy. Once again, I felt that I had really been seen, again validating my sanity.

GOOD MORNING: A holocaust-themed movie has long been an ambition of Arthur Hiller's – and he's now working on one. Tentatively titled "The Waltonsteins," it's based on the story of two holocaust survivors who met in Ottawa, married and had two children. The father was so paranoid about the holocaust, and what happened to its children, he and his wife and the children converted to Catholicism in Canada. How they regained their identify and the participation of the Catholic Church in their reconversion are parts of the drama. Hiller learned of the story when it was being performed in a one-woman show in Ottawa by Frannie Sheridan. She and partner Pat Bermel are now writing the screenplay. Hiller would make it as a lower-budgeted indie ... Those who have seen "Wag the Dog" have no doubt that Dustin Hoffman's portrayal of Hollywood producer Stanley Mott is a takeoff of Robert Evans. But director Barry Levinson says, "It could be a half dozen others with similar hairdos and big glasses. As a matter of fact, we switched to those glasses at the last minute, because of the hairdo." As for trying to make him a character designed to humor Hollywood's "insiders," Levinson noted that would be "too simplistic, Besides, there is no 'inside' Hollywood anymore: Everyone is savvy about the movie business, with entertainment shows airing everywhere. Example: when my mother in Boca Raton asks me what the weekend grosses were, I know there is no more Hollywood inside!" Of course most "insiders" (except Levinson) saw a gag reel made during filming of "The Marathon Man" at Par, where stars Laurence Olivier, Roy Scheider and Hoffman all did takeoff imitations of the pic's producer, Robert Evans. Evans says that reel is now "locked up" but added he was "flattered" that Hoffman was reviving his portrayal. P.S. Evans has not yet seen the movie. "For the first time in a long time, I have (had?) nothing to complain about." He's working on his book "Seduction" and, with Scott Rudin, readying the new version of "The Out-Of-Towners."

Hiller works on 'Waltonsteins'
By Army Archerd

https://variety.com/1997/voices/columns/hiller-works-on-waltonsteins-1116678077/

I awoke balled up in the middle of my empty queen-sized bed. I flipped over, then using the sheets, made a wrinkly snow angel while singing "Hallelujah".

I was meeting Arthur later that day. He had come to Vancouver to spitball ideas with me and Pat, for further development on the screenplay. During our last phone call, Arthur had referred to Pat as my "special other" so I let him know that our relationship was platonic. I treasured my friendship with Pat and absolutely knew that although we were not meant to be romantic partners, initiating the screenplay together was a powerful creation. As there are no coincidences, while working on the script together, Pat had been inspired to research his own heritage. Auspiciously he discovered his own Jewish heritage.

Arthur, Pat and I had agreed to give the project the working title 'Never Tell Anyone', a recurring phrase which I had written into my father's dialogue in both the play and screenplay.

First, Arthur and his adorable wife, Gwennie, took me to lunch. They had been married for decades. Both were petite. When they sat, they held hands and gazed wordlessly into each other's eyes. This seemed to be a complete anomaly for a Hollywood couple who had been married for longer than thirty seconds.

I piped up, "I'm so inspired with how romantic you two are with each other!"

"We work at it," they answered in sync. "We've known each other since grammar school," Arthur added. "We've been asked to give workshops about romance on cruise ships, but Gwennie doesn't like public speaking."

Gwennie nodded, smiling, as she ran her hand through his beautiful white mane of hair.

"Well, I hope that your magic will help me find the right boyfriend!"

Arthur smiled. "He'll find you."

"He will," Gwennie added with her sweet voice. "You have time. You're just a baby! Forty? Please!"

Gwennie left after lunch and we headed to Pat's place. It was riveting having Arthur dissect our script and suggest additions. He liked many of our ideas and agreed that the anecdote about my having worked as a stripper for six weeks would be a powerful feature.

"Should you ever decide to strip again, and this time tour Beverly Hills, I'll be sure to come to see you!" he joked.

I took a moment to take in my life. It was heavenly working with this great man. Already well into his seventies, he suddenly informed us that it was naptime and promptly fell asleep on Pats couch.

In between working with him, I flew around performing *The Waltonsteins* internationally. At one point, the Yiddish theater expert Avi Hoffman took my project under his wing. I had hoped we would further the play together because not only was Avi an accomplished showman, but his Jewish Theater Arts company had been one of the sponsors for my O-1 Writer/Actor visa. He directed a version of the show and further translated the Yiddish I'd heard my parents speaking at home, often during their arguments.

Arthur helped to get my play booked in a range of theaters through writing letters of support to Artistic Directors. His influence was also paramount in my having obtained an O-1 Writer/Actor visa. I wished that I'd had more clout to return the favor. Although he was wildly accomplished in the movie industry, he shared that due to his advanced age he was often dismissed as a has-been by Hollywood. He even told me that although he wanted to direct my film, I might have more luck getting it

---

Arthur Hiller

GOLDEN QUILL
P.O. Box 21377
Beverly Hills, CA 90213

Phone: (310) 246-0451
Fax: (310) 276-2068

RE: *"Never Tell Anyone"*

To Whom It May Concern:

I first saw Frannie Sheridan perform her dark and humorous one person show, *The Waltonsteins,* in Canada in front of a packed 800-seat audience. She moved them and me to tears and laughter, expertly performing a range of characters from her incredible family story.

Although I am not attached to direct it, Frannie has worked under my tutelage to build her powerful story of a search for identity into a screenplay. *"Never Tell Anyone"* is the name of her well woven full-length, multi-cast feature film script. It's unique and different in story and style, and yet it keeps you emotionally involved.

I suspect you'll feel the same way when you read it and that you'll want to be part of her 'support team' to take this from script to screen.

Sincerely,
Arthur Hiller

made with a younger director. He said that he wouldn't get in the way of the production if I decided to go with someone else. I couldn't imagine doing so. But, for that reason, he was sensitive to include the phrase "although I am not attached to direct" in all associated documents.

I spent many years working with Arthur, together with different screenwriting partners. He was consistently excited about the work and his warm, longtime assistant Brenda coordinated meetings including with the networks and forwarded the script to potential producers and stars. I loved spending time at his stunning bungalow-style mansion in Beverly Hills, which he referred to as 'my humble shack", purchased after making 'Love Story'.

One day, we sat in Arthur's living room staring wordlessly at the collection of totem poles in his backyard. Earlier that day, we'd met with his agent Phil Gersh, creator of one of the largest Hollywood film and television agencies, 'The Gersh Agency'. Phil had put the screen-play through the studios but as much as they loved the story, nobody had bitten. Arthur had often said that it was tricky getting a film made in Hollywood which had as much heart as entertainment value. I recalled reading about how challenging it had been for Stephen Spielberg to get 'Schindler's List' made. We had recently threaded content to do with my stripping escapade into the script, hoping it would give the work the necessary current edge to excite a powerful producer.

We decided to grab some lunch to change the mood. Gwennie offered to make meatballs, but then Arthur suggested it'd be less work for her if he took us to lunch at 'The Hamburger Hamlet'.

En route, he told us that he was playing hooky from his friends because normally he met with a number of them who were *big machers* --important people, who were in the film and television comedy industry, for ongoing lunches there. They called themselves the '*Alta Kakers Club*' --Old Timer's Club. Arthur said they would likely be lunching there now.

Well, he wasn't kidding when he had referred to *"big machers"*. When we walked in, the table full of iconic men happily yelled his name. "What are you doing here, Arthur?" yipped Sid Caeser. "Thought you had a meeting with Phil and the gal you're working on the Jewish film with." Then he looked at me playfully batting his eyes. "Oh hello!"

Arthur introduced us. "I know who you are!" I said giggling.

"Well, I'll be damned!" said Mr. Caeser, "Cuz I know who you are too!" and warmly shook my hand. I was almost rendered speechless as Arthur then introduced me to Hal Kanter, Carl Reiner, Monty Hall, Rocky Kalish and Gary Owens amongst other legendary geniuses.

After lunch which I barely touched as I was on sensory overload, I had to vamoose to the airport. That evening, I was scheduled to perform the revision of my original play *The Waltonteins*. I had recreated the show so that it was more of a character-driven portrayal and splashed it with additional humor. I called the new work *Confessions of a Jewish Shiksa*. It was being directed by a sassy, theatrically accomplished New Yorker, named Shari Upbin, in a stunning Miami Beach theater called 'The Colony'. My unstoppable Publicist Tandi Wilder informed me that afterwards I was going to be awarded a mayoral proclamation. Whether I performed the piece in Canada or the states, the humor which I had mined from the cast of dark characters in my new solo show seemed to allow viewers just enough respite to appreciate the depth of the drama. Only a week prior, I had received my first proclamation (key to the city) after performing my play in West Palm Beach at 'The Kravis Center'. After the Mayor of West Palm Beach handed me the certificate in front of the audience, I had noticed that my name was misspelled. It was written as 'Fannie' instead of Frannie. Patting my bottom, I shared that error with the crowd, and then quipped; "…so, on behalf of both my *tuchas* --bottom, and myself, I want to thank you for this beautiful award!"

The City of West Palm Beach

Congratulations

Fannie Sheridan

In Recognition of your Accomplishments and Outstanding Performance as a performer/writer of your unique multi-character solo show: Confessions of a Jewish Shiksa…Dancing on Hitler's Grave.

April 13, 2010

Lois J. Frankel, Mayor

"WEST PALM BEACH WASN'T ONLY CRAZY ABOUT MY SHOW, APPARENTLY, BUT ALSO CRAZY ABOUT MY "TUCHAS!"

Passing through a rough neighborhood during the cab-ride to the theater caused me to recall the first time I'd been naked onstage at the strip club, when I'd felt carefree for a few delightful moments. What if I could feel that level of openness and spontaneity while clothed, even performing my one-person show? I had already experienced sporadic creative freedom onstage while executing characters, especially when I sensed the audiences engagement. Would imagining that feeling of bliss prior to coming onstage help to literally emotionally set the scene? That was what acting was, wasn't it? Pre-paving emotionally? So, why couldn't I "act" the part of a carefree performer?

I promised to soothe myself into that joyous emotional state before every show. What the heck, I would make it part of my practice to immerse myself in feeling wonderful before communicating with anyone, offstage as well. Since I had spent so much of my life expecting negative situations, I knew it would take some practice to maintain feeling good but I was determined. *Shivers.* I knew I had hit on something powerful.

Once we reached the city of Miami, I was stunned to see the following billboard. I had never had a billboard dedicated to my work. It was better than sex.

CERTIFICATE OF RECOGNITION
Awarded to
FRANNIE SHERIDAN

In recognition of your accomplishments as a performer/writer of your
unique multi-character solo show - Confessions of a Jewish Shiksa.
Your story of the Sigal family, Holocaust survivors hiding their heritage
behind the cloak of Catholicism is a powerful one.
The City of Miami Beach recognizes your talents and the importance of
your incredible family story.

March 13, 2010

Matti Herrera Bower
Mayor

MIAMIBEACH

So, what does a nice Jewish girl do after she comes out of the knish closet? Join J-Date….and after date #5,431, I met my future husband. I was instantly smitten by Dani's lively camel-shaped eyes and his exuberant, unedited persona. His Sephardic (I'm Ashkenazi) Israeli temperament included a warm open laugh, and a very protective edge, as well as a complete lack of volume control. Sephardic Israelis are like human megaphones! Heads up: If you spend time with us, and notice that when you speak to me, I ignore you, it's not because I'm a snob; I'm wearing ear plugs. It's great; I haven't had to use a Q-Tip since I met him. I'm telling you! Once he was asked to speak at a funeral and was cited for waking the dead.

Anyway, you can always tell the difference between us generally more soft-spoken Ashkenazi (Eastern-European) Jews and Sephardic (Hispanic, Middle Eastern) Jews, particularly Sephardic Israelis. They are pretty much like any other Sephardic Jew, except imagine that the Sephardic Jew just guzzled six cups of espresso and stuck a box of firecrackers up their *tuchas* --bottom! They act like they're always ready to conquer. Especially when it comes to food. Getting a table at Starbucks with Dani is like a military operation.

The moment we walk in he gets really hyper and shouts, (Israeli accent) "Secure the table! Hurry! Go-go-go before anyone claims the territory! Get to the front of the line before someone orders the last blueberry muffin! Go!"

The last thing he needs is more coffee. However, many afternoons Dani and I frequent our local Palm Beach Starbucks. A family who is widely known to be well-heeled, comes in regularly. The Barista's, who we've befriended, divulged that the parents have been caught on camera displaying bizarre antics. First, they order food, gather it from the pick-up counter, eat it, and then hide the wrappings at the bottom of the garbage can. Then, they inform the Barista's that they have not yet received their order and are given a 'replacement'. Additionally, their kids have a habit of glaring at adults for uncomfortably long periods of time. Dani and I ignore them entirely. But one day, after I'd found us a seat, the kids leaned on the counter a few feet away attempting to stare me down. I got up for thirty seconds to tell Dani, who was standing in line perched to order, what I wanted to drink. When I returned there was a small pile of torn dark paper on my chair. The kids who were now seated outside on the other side of the window from where I sat, were laughing along with their parents, all of them looking at me. At this point Dani comes over with the drinks and observes what's happening. He sits as I mouthed 'Very funny!' The kooky family looked away.

Now, at the worst of times when I was living for a week on a box of spaghetti, I wouldn't try a trick like that. And these delightful human specimens have more gold and diamonds on their bodies than Tiffany's has in their window. So, now we've decided to pay attention.

Later that afternoon when the kids put some crap on somebody else's seat, Dani calls them over. He shows them his cell phone and says, "I have a video of what you just did. And if you do it again, I'm going to call the police and they'll make you clean the toilets here with your tongue."

They run to their table and say something to their father. He comes over to our table in a huff and says, "What did you just say to my son?"

Dani begins, "I told him that" --

And I butt in with "My husband is very humble. He would never say it himself, but he told your son how lucky he was to have such fine moral examples in his life like you and your wife."

Then Dani gives him his crazy eye stare. (Every Israeli is taught the demented eye stare before they're taught how to strip and assem-

214

ble an Uzi in under a minute. If confronted by the enemy, you give him the look and he thinks he's looking in a mirror and moves on.) The father immediately groups his family together, and they make a speedy exit. Shortly thereafter one of the Baristas comes over and places a package of our favorite chocolate-covered cookies on our table and says, "With the compliments and gratitude of the staff."

People often ask how it is that Dani and I spend so much time together and seem to get along so well. I always give the same answer – Dani's strong Israeli accent is our sexy secret because for all the years we've been together, I've hardly understood a thing he's said! And although I'm obviously joking, as my dear Papa would say, "There's a little truth in every joke!" But being a humorist, I say, there's a little joke in every truth, exemplified in the following case of Dani's accent.

We entered a local establishment for lunch. After Dani and I discussed that we would order kale salad, I headed to the bathroom. When I returned to the table, the waiter brought over what appeared to be chicken salads.

"Why did you order us chicken, I asked for kale?" I asked Dani.

He turned to the waiter speaking with his beautiful Israeli accent; "That's what I order from you! *Quail* salad! What eez thees?"

And so, the story of the freshness of our marriage prevails.

Although we have a lot of fun together over the years, I began experiencing physical challenges. Repeatedly reenacting the darkly dramatic components of the show about my family had taken a toll on my body.

For the first few decades, publicly sharing outlawed family secrets in my play ranging from my grandmother's murder to my parents tortured marriage had been therapeutic and riveting. But once I had healed that piece of my life, the experience shifted, and reliving the sadness over and over onstage had begun to feel as if I was repeatedly ripping a scab open. But bookings were plentiful, and I felt an obligation to see them through for a few more years. The emotional cost contributed to sarcoma in my uterus. It was as if my body was literally dying to birth something life-giving. However, the experience was ultimately an enormous gift. It taught me to ever more deeply make my feelings a priority, no matter what. I am now entirely healthy and have been for years.

I still share my family story as a performance piece, but primarily from a light-hearted, humorous perspective which barely touches on pathos. It feels heartwarming and winning to me and I love lifting audiences.

Although I emerged from the night of the inter-generational wormhole, I still struggle with one aspect of DNA inherited from my Viennese father, for which I continue to blame him; specifically, the "pastry gene" referred to early in the book. Luckily, Dani shares my dessert addiction, and we turned it into a business. We had known for a while that we wanted to do something on camera involving food. But it took us a while to embrace dessert as the specific type of food. Initially, since we eat healthy not to mention that hubby has a Mediterranean Organic Food Business, it was a no-brainer to go in that direction. I pitched Whole Foods a TV pilot called Frannie's Wacky Healthy Food Show, which they sponsored, and we filmed in their Palm Beach Gardens, Florida studio kitchen in front of a live audience. They applauded its entertainment value but waffled on moving ahead. So, we launched into a youtube series called The Sweethearts during which we share humorous shenanigans while reviewing desserts. It led to us costarring in a series of TV commercials for Aztil air conditioning playing ourselves as Dessert Reviewers, which airs on CBS/FOX. We then developed a concept for an American-Canadian TV series which I cowrote with David Wolinsky. It will costar Mark Breslin, founder and owner of YukYuks comedy chain featured with other comedy greats in the TV documentary *When Jews Were Funny,* and producer for the TV series *The Late Show with Joan Rivers.* The project also costars celebrity photographer Robert Zuckerman (Will Smith calls him Picasso. Jerry Bruckheimer, Denzel Washington and Michael Bay vie to have him on their film sets. And Arnold Schwarzenegger introduced him to Bill Clinton as "the best photographer I have ever worked with") and Wendy Hammers (a seasoned actress and standup comic who has appeared on Seinfeld, Curb Your Enthusiasm and The Sopranos.)

In the meantime, we are having a great time inspiring audiences to be playful while fressing --eating up a sweet storm once a week in our youtube series which garnered us a laurel for BEST COMEDY WEBS SERIES 2020 at The Palm Beach International

Mini Film Festival. But by far the accomplishment I am most proud of, is having taught my Mediterranean-tempered Israeli-Egyptian husband to meditate.

When we decided to wed, our oceanside venue was of course chosen largely due to it serving one of the most sumptuous chocolate ganache cakes in Florida. I had hoped that Arthur would co-officiate our nuptials together with our Rabbi. Sadly, he was too frail to fly here from Beverly Hills, and instead gave us a generous gift as was his nature.

Over the years, Arthur's support greatly fueled my ambition to continue to ripen my play. After one performance in Baltimore (this is the one which had been backed by Senators), I was given a tour of the capitol; "That's where Monica and Bill did their thing!" they giggled, pointing through the window to the "scene of the crime". As I referenced in the prologue: Rules are rules. Some things are never forgotten. My father taught me that. But memory is shaped by perspective. So now, when I think about my fathers' funeral, which was attended by the entire Viennese Chassidic community since his beloved grandfather, the Rabbi Izi Hirsch Beutel was a treasured member, it feels more beautiful than sad to me. Hopefully, some things may be forgiven. Which is why I have written this book and disclosed my past sins. I forgave Monica the moment Bill bragged about dipping his cigar. And she never even took off her clothes in public. So, I may be asking a lot, but I'm hoping folks will accord me the same kindness. But even if you don't it's okay.

As a child, having been taught that I was viciously negatively judged by the world birthed a powerful desire to feel love while connecting to all people despite their opinion of me. Plus, on some level, as a former Catholic who has earned the ability to confess, I do feel that all my sins have been expatiated. But when you cut through the *drek*--shit, there was never anything that needed to be forgiven in the first place. Shame and guilt were just something we fabulously screwy fearful humans thought up to control each other with. And for those of you who don't agree, as a Jewish woman who inherited an ability to lay on the guilt from the best --my dear Momma, let me spread a little your way. Momma would say things like; "It's my fault you don't clean up after yourselves! I'm to blame. You're just children and don't know better. Oy, I'm the one who should be punished!" And then us kids would immediately wash our dishes even if we were mid-eating and make our beds before getting out of them. So, if you're watching Momma, I listened and learned.

I sensed both of my parents' spirits with me the day Dani and I were married by our Rabbi Resnick of Palm Beach, on the sand, next to the ocean. A roving violinist serenaded us as we walked towards the group of just under forty guests. It meant a great deal to me that as far as family, my wedding was attended by my eldest brother, his common-law partner Caren, and daughter Jess, as well as Uncle Gerd's daughter Judy.

I now felt like the war inside of me was finally really over. Not just from having married my beloved, but that the Jewish wedding rituals hadn't triggered much sadness. And it wasn't only that we were two people with mutual intent to create a happy home. We had the skills to pull it off! Having both come from very different backgrounds, both rife with various kinds of anxiety, we made it a priority to refine our emotional coping skills so that we were almost always able to navigate challenges without feeling crappy. We never acted phony but instead allowed ourselves to climb up the emotional ladder with the goal of feeling as good as authentically possible. That practiced focus allowed us to literally repaint the landscape of our lives on an ongoing basis. My world was no longer black and white.

I glanced at my relatives huddled around us which made me think about other descendants of the Holocaust. I said a silent prayer imagining that they too were able to find a way to get past PTSD and color their lives with joy. When I married and stood under the *chuppah* --a canopy, in my turquoise mermaid gown holding a bouquet of orange tiger lilies to match Dani's silk outfit, and heard the glass break when he stomped on it with his foot, for me it symbolized not the night of broken glass that so terrorized the Jews of Europe, but the shattering of my old fear and shame and grief.

The most common regret heard from people at the ends of their lives is "I wish I hadn't cared so much what others thought of me".

IMMENSE THANKS TO:
My treasured husband Dani, my parents and all those who came before, my brothers and sisters (on both warring familial "sides")

and in alphabetical order of surnames: Pat Bermel, Heather Cohen, Janet Corne and Family, Diana Dent, Lynna Goldhar-Smith, Arthur Hiller, Kerri John, Brenda Glazerman Knight, Andrea Hughes, Shelley Page, Albert Palombo, Karen Propp, Heather Sandvold-Kavadas, Susan Weidman Schneider, Susan Schnur, Marilee Sigal, Benson Simmonds, Marylee Stephenson, David Spanner, Jessica Vanderveen, David Wolinsky members of writing critique groups...we are ALL co-creating! If I've forgotten to mention anyone, please know that I failed to mention the assholes. Hey – there's a "little asshole" inside all of us if we want to activate it. Truthfully, I appreciate every single experience I had - even those that were kakapoopoo. Because without them, I wouldn't be right here with you. Thank you and love to everyone and everything in our magnificent world.

CPSIA information can be obtained
at www.ICGtesting.com
Printed in the USA
FSHW022028161121
86230FS